ECHOES OF NO THING

Fig. 1. Hieronymus Bosch, *Ship of Fools* (1490–1500)

First published in 2018 by punctum books, Earth, Milky Way.
https://punctumbooks.com

ISBN-13: 978-1-950192-01-4 (print)
ISBN-13: 978-1-950192-02-1 (ePDF)

LCCN: 2018968574
Library of Congress Cataloging Data is available from the Library of Congress

Book design: Vincent W.J. van Gerven Oei
Cover photograph: Nico Jenkins, "Il Passo del Monte Moro," 2015

HIC SVNT MONSTRA

ECHOES
OF NO THING
Thinking between Heidegger and Dōgen

Nico Jenkins

Contents

For Jessica,
who let me do my best,
and who believed I could,
always.

Acknowledgments

This project would not have been possible but for the help of many.

I wish to thank, first and foremost, and with devotion and love, Jessica Kerwin Jenkins, who, as already mentioned, always believed I could do my best, and gave me the freedom and space to try. Without her, nothing happens.

I wish to also thank Robert Brewer Young, who has walked beside me from the Tenderloin to the Lower East Side to the Marais, and who, gently at times, and harshly at others, queried who I was and what I believed, and in turn invited me to do the same to him. With Robert, I wish to acknowledge the late Hal Sarf, whose Saturday morning classes on thinking led me, for the first time, into the circle of wonder, as well as Ray Mondini, at the San Francisco Art Institute, whose pedagogy of passionate madness drove me to think I could (wonder).

I thank also both my parents, Nancy Harmon Jenkins and Loren Jenkins, without whom I could not have been who I am.

I am also indebted to my colleagues at the various institutions where I have taught, and who believed in me before I did. To both Husson University and the University of Maine especially, I owe a debt of gratitude.

In addition, without the support of my advisor Christopher Fynsk at the European Graduate School, who gave me the space and encouragement to read and explore, as well as Judith Balso and Alain Badiou who took me to dinner and listened, none of this could have happened. Indeed, without the University in Exile — and its mad, mad hatter, Wolfgang Schirmacher — little occurs.

Finally, I wish to thank the tireless vision and labor of all at punctum books, especially Eileen Joy, whose relentless pursuit of the para-academic and open access is an inspiration and critique to all, and to my editor, Vincent van Gerven Oei, who has both spoken with me and carried me through this process — sometimes patiently, and at other times with delightful scorn. My debt to you is constant.

…they're going to abandon me, there will be the silence, for a moment, for a good few moments, or it will be mine, the lasting one, that didn't last, that still lasts, it will be I, you must go on, I can't go on, you must go on, I'll go on, you must say words, as long as there are any, until they find me, until they say me, strange pain, strange sin, you must go on, perhaps its done already, perhaps they have said me already, perhaps they have carried me to the threshold of my story, before the door that opens on my story, that would surprise me, if it opens, it will be I, it will be the silence, where I am, I don't know, I'll never know, in the silence you don't know, you must go on, I can't go on, I'll go on.
— Samuel Beckett, *The Unnamable*

Introduction

*Younger Man: In waiting, we are purely
"present" as literally "waiting-toward."*

*Older Man: And nothing else. We are this so purely that from
nowhere else does something stand over against us, to which we
could cling and into which we would still want to escape.*

*Younger Man: In waiting, we are in such a manner as though we
were to have passed away unnoticed and unnamed — not there
for all who still await this or that and still expect from this or that
something for themselves, Waiting is in essence otherwise than all
awaiting and expecting, which are basically unable to wait.*
— Martin Heidegger, *Country Path Conversations*

*Entirely worlding the entire world with the whole world is thus called
penetrating exhaustively. To immediately manifest the bodying of
the tall golden Buddha with the body of the tall golden Buddha
as the arising of religious mind, as practice, as enlightenment, as
nirvana — that is being, that is time. One does nothing but penetrate
entire time as entire being. There is nothing remaining left over.*
— Dōgen, "Uji"

John Cage's *4′33″* remains an echo, a repetition of the space of
silence and all silence entails. Performed for the first time by

pianist David Tudor in 1954 during a piano recital in Wood-stock, New York, it asks of the performer to sit at the piano, and to "perform" a piece of music. Tudor interpreted the instructions Cage had written and sat at the piano, with the lid raised, for two minutes and twenty-three seconds. He then closed the lid, checked his watch, and raised it again. He sat for another two minutes, and then left the stage. Whereas the music created during a conventional concert, in effect, banishes the sound of the world by filling a discrete space with a sequence of pre-selected notes, Cage's *4'33"* — performed *as* silence — beckons sound forth, to come forward, to intrude or even to rest in the space. Sound, noise, voice, music are all made present through silence's *be*-coming. An echo of silence shelters and holds itself as silence as a vessel or form holds itself. In the destruction of silence, noise creates the piece. Noise presencing is allowed to be revealed through the absenting of action, through the absenting of the intentional making of a note, of composed, ordered music. In English, the verb "to make" remains the same whether one is making a building or work of art. In Latin, however, we can separate the two terms; *facio,* which refers to the making of material things, is contrasted to *creo* which, as its name implies, refers to the creation of a thing. Creation carries with it a semblance of the divine, something which is primordial, un-made. Allowing noise to come forward as an incipient irruption into the silence, to *be*-come, is an unmaking of its original form. Though criticized as a sham and a farce at the time, *4'33"* has become an iconic[1] piece of "music" and inscribes perfectly a silence between words (without language) as the space between notes, between intentional noises. What is important about the piece, however, is not its shock value, but rather the attempt Cage made to say, or to think, silence within sounds, to think the unsignable within an architecture of signs, to say — or give voice to — the unsayable, that which refuses to be said, and

---

1   There are numerous videos online "recreating" the silence(s) of Cage's *4'33"*, including a death metal version by Dead Territory, https://youtu.be/voqC-QSDAcn8.

which emerges in the space between, and which makes noise qua noise impossible.

Heidegger's Echoes

Like the dynamic silences in *4'33"*, the world itself seems to be defined by the movement of objects within the lacunal spaces of nothing, objects that are both in relation to each other and to *no*[special]*thing*. Martin Heidegger describes this movement as a resonating, or the play between withdrawal and unconcealment, a resonating which allows for the "essential occurrence of Being [*Seyn*] in the abandonment of being."[2] Like the anticipated withdrawal of formal composition in *4'33"*, Heidegger describes a space between, the abandonment of the absolute in favor of the unconcealing of that which remains covered. Like sounds emerging in silence, things come to be in their absence(s) and withdrawal. The phenomenological appearance of the object in the world both shields itself as it appears and disappears from the stage in its coming to be. Everything seems, on one level, to be in doubt, and like *The Republic*'s grand puppet show, in which the assumed reality of the phenomenon quite literally disappears epistemologically up what could be termed a rabbit hole, so our attempt to understand the object similarly resists definition, defying language even to make sense of a senseless world. Like the sounds that come to be during *4'33"*, unrehearsed, uncoordinated, un-curated, chaotic, and cluttered, so things, and even beings, suddenly loom large in our world, unpredictably defying absolute definition as quickly as they come to be. What is a cloud in the sky against the autumn leaves of a yellowed tree? What is the ocean under this sky, against this land? And, more importantly, what do we, as beings, mean under this sky and in front of this sea, and, in Levinasian terms at least, as beings "here below"? For Heidegger, beings in the world take

---

2   Martin Heidegger, *Contributions to Philosophy (Of the Event),* trans. Richard Rojcewicz and Daniela Vallega-Neu (Bloomington: Indiana University Press, 2012), 85.

place in the house of language. But the object (for me if not for Heidegger) — the thing in itself — incessantly, even violently, resists definition, resists naming. So how to describe that which remains unnameable?

While *4'33"* is clearly a rehearsed movement (even the movement of non-movement), an act of pure artifice and theater, there exists this play of emergence and withdrawal — perceptive and palpable — within the world, outside of the hall (concert or otherwise). It acts as a stain of being, a trace of beings' withdrawal. This essay will seek to understand the play Heidegger describes between things and beings, and beings and beings. Using as guides the initially improbable bedfellows of Heidegger and the Zen Patriarch Eihei Dōgen of 12th-century Japan to help explicate these inexplicable movements, it will attempt to chart the space — the silences — between things in an effort to understand the things themselves. As a traversal across disciplines and cultures, time and place, this thinking will anticipate conflicts and disturbances within the joining of two distinct thinkers. This play of *be*-coming can seem Heraclitean (*as something is coming to be, it is becoming something other than*) in its movement; it is also, with Dōgen, *within* the actual movement of things themselves. Dōgen writes, *even though you study movement, it is not what you think it is.* To Martin Heidegger, the world worlds in the pulsing movement of withdrawal and unconcealment of being, and, echoing again the movement of water, describes truth as *alētheia,* drawing on, and contrasting the root-word — *lēthē* — which refers originally to something covered up, concealed, or latent and is symbolized by mythological river Lethe, the river of forgetting. Language speaks, says Heidegger. *Die Sprache spricht.* Language, to Heidegger, resides in the house of being, yet too often this language fails to bring being forth, fails to name and summon that which comes forth. So often, we do not allow language to speak — whether to us or to others, or even to itself — we *fail* to listen. Instead we *speak* the language, we inscribe the evental phenomenon with words, and we cover it with a saying, a chattering, which, though it claims an authority to explain and describe, is instead a babble of noise rather than a listening — not for words but for a presencing of world — and which acts as a cover, or as a fogging of the world, and the word.

Christopher Fynsk, in writing on Blanchot's *Infinite Conversation,* describes an alternative to "the speech of the everyday" (which is what language all too commonly remains) when he describes Blanchot's desire for something "entirely different, a cold interruption, the rupture of a circle."[3] Fynsk writes that this interruption is "to will something that communicates or affirms itself in that break."[4] It is this rupture of the shared quotidian space where language as language seems to fail and which both Heidegger and Dōgen, as we shall see, are directing us towards. The interruption is a violence in that it destroys the veneer of commonality, yet precisely because shared commonality is a mere veneer, it "allows" for another truth, an originary experience of the event of *alētheia* to emerge. This interruption serves to illustrate the vital contrast between *lēthē* and its a-privative counterpart, *alētheia. Lēthē* is the covered up, the forgotten meaning that rests below the surface; as its negation, *alētheia* becomes that uncovering, that restitution of the original sense, that calling forth that the practice of thinking *as practice* allows. This is an explosive interruption. In bringing the practice of thinking forth, it, in Fynsk's treatment, opens "the fragmenting force of an infinite conversation and to will disappearance, in friendship, from the common space of achieved understanding."[5]

The world is made of things, it is filled with objects sitting in near and distant connection and relation to each other. Language, used properly (responsibly), binds these relations and allows us to make sense of them (*if we can make sense*). Language speaks and in speaking makes the world apparent, gives form to the phenomenon. According to Heidegger, we dwell as language in the house of being. Language, again used responsibly, creates

---

3   This is from Blanchot's *Infinite Conversation* cited in Christopher Fynsk, *Last Steps: Maurice Blanchot's Exilic Writing* (New York: Fordham University Press, 2013), 77.

4   Ibid.

5   Ibid., 78.

order in the world; it controls and makes *ready* the world. But language, used another way, irresponsibly though not destructively, sought not as a unifier but as a disruptive, irruptive force, as a force that withdraws instead of suffocates, allows for things to be, to come forth, to assume their own selves, and not the projected self. This, however, is a language that does not come from a subject, that does not make (*facio*) and order in the way music, composed and rendered, orders noise, or in the way words on a page order things, but rather language as a primordial, originary force allows to be, or lets be (*gelassen*) in the world. We are dealing now with two different languages; we dwell in two houses. The first is the language of logic, of the ordered, controlled world of scientific, rational thinking. The second language (and still a language) draws from the primordial ground of worlds worlding, of things coming to be; it by neccessity must remain on the edge of thinking, resting on the outer fringes of thinking and always seeking a further interruption. This language is never still and always perpetually reopened. Objects come to be without language; mountains become, as do oceans and beings, before language (and will come after) but it is language, used both responsibly and otherwise, used to describe and order but also to recognize, experience, which sets them in motion in *our* world, which make them of significance to *us*. The languages of the sciences delineate and order, but primordial language *sets free* objects into the world, allows things to *be*-come of the world. Without language, how does a thing — in the world — or in our world, come to be understood? And, perhaps more importantly, how do we (as things, as beings) come to be understood to ourselves? Can we understand, perceive without language? Can we, as pure being, encounter world without language?

Not only does language always seem to fail us in the world, objects in the world fail us as well. With, or through, language, objects inevitably seem to withdraw to a further horizon of intelligibility. An object in one place seems always ready to relocate itself to another, and indeed does always withdraw from us knowing it entirely. (By objects, it is important to note that I include, with coffee cups, jet airplanes, computers, clouds and

scenic overlooks, also thoughts, ideas, conceptions, beliefs, ide-
ologies, environments, universes and universities, and even beings themselves.)

How are we to speak about this world then, this *logos* of con-
nections and relations, beliefs, and things, bound and possibly
unbound by language? This essay will explore obliquely the use
of language, and, more importantly, seek an attempt to chart
what it is we experience when we experience things (through
language). How are we to describe such a world, if, as Heidegger
argues, we acknowledge — and name — its continual withdrawal if its always already something else as well as language's in-
nate failure to be able to apprehend it in its withdrawal? How
do we describe the being of be-ings (all beings, all things) as
Being while allowing for things to continue to *lassen,* or let be?
How do we talk about things, exist with things, allow ourselves
to be let into (*eingelassen*) objects that are already withdrawn?
How do we avoid making (*plattō*) a world of descriptions and
concepts on top of a world that exists before language? How are
we to come to know the world, to exist, not in a web of notions,
or behind a brutally effective scrim of names, but in its originary
sense. Heidegger asks if such a language would say anything at
all? With Beckett, as with Heidegger, we feel we must say words
"as long as there are any,"[6] but what are words in the wreckage
of language, in the gap between saying and the thing? What are
words in the irruption and interruption of being's *be-*coming?
And yet, silence (acquiescence) is not an option either. *We must
say words. We must say words as a practice.*

One of the central texts that this study will draw on is *Country Path Conversations,* a collection of three "conversations" that
Heidegger wrote in 1944–45, but which were not published until
1995, nearly twenty years after his death. In the third dialogue,
"Evening Conversations," Heidegger describes an exchange taking place within a Russian forest in a prisoner-of-war camp during the closing days of a devastating war. The war is, of course,
World War II, and Heidegger's two sons were then missing, pre-

---

6   Samuel Beckett, *The Unnamable* (New York: Grove Press, 1958), 179.

sumed to be imprisoned in the East. The dialogue is not between brothers, however, but between two men — one young and one old — who describe, among other things, the process of waiting and of waiting's *Gelassenheit,* or releasement. Waiting, for the prisoners, is a waiting on no thing (as opposed to nothing which would still be a *some*thing), it is an attending *towards* a pure nothing. Only through this attuned, attentive waiting — Heidegger at one point refers to it as a meditation — can "what is healing draw near." This drawing near is a drawing near of being to beings, a healing in a world of beings violently separated from being itself. The prisoners' conversation is a description of both the stupefying boredom of their imprisonment — the sense of endless awaiting, day giving way to night, work to sleep — and, at the same time, the absolute freedom of being that a recognition of one's captivity, whether behind barbed wire or as a fundamental condition of life as an existential subject, allows. "To simply wait," the Younger Man says, "as though this compliance were to consist in waiting; and to wait so long, as though waiting would have to outlast death."[7] In Heidegger's words, the clearing, which happens literally within the vast swathes of the Russian forest, is attained through "pure waiting," and not "awaiting." It is objectless and waits for no thing, not even Nothing. Rather, waiting is defined by the Younger Man as "to wait on that which answers pure waiting [...] waiting is letting come."[8] This waiting is a practice, an attunement, towards a "letting come" of no thing as rationally ordered phenomena, but rather the evental unconcealment of an authentic event of Being.

Waiting, then, is a letting appear of what can appear, or an allowing to presence of something seemingly not there, something resolutely withdrawn (but only temporarily). As the Younger Man puts it in "Evening Conversations," that period of waiting is the period in which, while waiting for nothing but what is to come, "we release things precisely into where we are

---

7   Martin Heidegger, *Country Path Conversations,* trans. Bret W. Davis (Bloomington: Indiana University Press, 2010), 140.

8   Ibid., 141.

[...] let ourselves into, namely into that in which we belong."[9] This process, which is at once a positive action, a doing (waiting) is also a stepping back, not in the form of passive submission, but rather in the form of letting things be. The notion that "waiting is letting come" is a releasement in the form of a letting be, of allowing things (beings, in the case of Heidegger) to rest in their own being.

But, in a form of double articulation familiar to Heidegger's readers, not only does *Gelassenheit* (releasement) allow things to "be," it also allows things to come, to emerge into their proper form, by allowing a thing its own disclosure. It creates a space, an opening within the noise of a world worlding. Allowing for a thing to come, whether a being or, as I will argue, a coffee cup, a football, or even Heidegger's apocryphal hammer, takes time. It is a practice; it requires a waiting, a waiting that is a listening and not a saying, a waiting that preserves and shelters, that observes and "holds" the space, refusing to fill it with the chatter of the everyday. As a practice, it is a waiting towards what is not known, but intimated; it is an anticipation of what is to come, but still unnamed. It is a waiting that is both profound and, possibly, according to the prisoners, a little boring. Boring is, for Heidegger, at least in his *Being and Time,* precisely the moment of our fundamental encounter with Dasein in its basic state.

That Heidegger chose to speak about the nature of language and of the object not through a linear text but through a dialogue, can't be ignored. A dialogue is a form of listening as much as it is a form of saying. It is a celebration of the multivocal plurality over the tyranny of the univocal author. It is a play between participants, both those written (named) as well as between author and reader; the dialogue exists *in between.* A dialogue, by its very nature is a series of interruptions and as such refuses to say the absolute and refers the reader to the gaps between the interlocutors, to the space between thoughts as much as to the actual sayings of the participants. Like Cage's *4'33"* in which the sounds of not playing allowed for echoes of

---

9   Ibid., 149.

nothing, in a dialogue, the space between utterances, the gaps, the stuttering of unuttered thoughts, the pauses, hold as much importance as that which is said. Silences, in effect, create the work as much as the babble and chatter of language.

Indeed, in two of the texts to be discussed in this essay, in the *Country Path Conversations* (which the above dialogue is taken from) as well as in *A Dialogue on Language,* Heidegger will limit himself to the use of dialogue; in another, *Contributions to Philosophy (Of the Event),* the hesitancy and wonder — the pure experiencing of thought — is dialogic in its rendering, disordered in its multivocality. More will be said of this further on, but it is important to note that even in Heidegger's essays, the mode or construct of the univocal is questioned to such a degree that the hegemony of the author — and thereby the said — is, to a large degree, broken down, subtracted, elided from the text itself, leaving a more pure space for thought, for things to emerge, for things to come. Heidegger's writing, especially in his later work, offers itself as pure thinking rather more than it seeks to declare a world; his thinking is meant as a gift and not as an absolute. The place where this thinking occurs, indeed where anything comes to be, Heidegger will call a "clearing" and a lightening (*Lichtung*); it is, for Heidegger, a place (though placeless) where, importantly, truth (*alētheia*) can for the first time come forward, can presence itself.

In "The End of Philosophy," Heidegger describes this opening, as a physical event; the forest clearing is not mere metaphor:

> The adjective *licht,* "open," is the same word as "light." To open something means: "to make something light, free and open, e.g. to make the forest free of trees at one place." The openness thus originating is the clearing. What is light in the sense of being free has nothing in common with the adjective "light," meaning bright — neither linguistically nor factually.[10]

10 Martin Heidegger, *Basic Writings,* ed. David Farrell Krell (New York: Harper & Row, 1977), 442.

For Heidegger, lightening means an opening: to shed light means to open a path through and into something. The opening which opens as a clearing operates as a clearing away, a making space, and becomes "the open region for everything that becomes present and absent."[11] What appears as be-coming becomes only through the clearing and opening of being becoming Being between things; like sounds between silences, beings become between.

The Unnecessary Necessary

That this waiting and this releasement should echo a vaguely Buddhistic sentiment should come as no surprise to the attuned reader of Heidegger. For much of his life, Heidegger watched, and was watched, by Taoist and Buddhist thinkers in Asia, primarily in Japan. Indeed, in "Evening Conversations," the dialogue between the prisoners ends with a retelling of an unattributed story of another dialogue between "two thinkers" of "Chinese philosophy." Heidegger doesn't disclose the identities of these two thinkers in his dialogue (the names of the two "escapes" the Older Man), but we know it to be a discourse between a Master Hui Tzu and, more notably, the great Taoist thinker Chuang Tzu of the 4th century BCE. Heidegger writes:

The one said: "You are talking about the unnecessary."
The other said: "A person must first have recognized the unnecessary before one can talk with him about the necessary. The earth is wide and large, and yet, in order to stand, the human needs only enough space to be able to put his foot down. But if directly next to his foot a crevice were to open up that dropped down into the underworld, then would the space where he stands still be of use to him?"
The one said: "It would be of no more use to him."

---

11   Ibid.

The other said: "From this the necessity of the unnecessary is clearly apparent."[12]

The necessity of the unnecessary is apparent as well to the two prisoners who struggle in their conversation with the concept of waiting on that which is a "waiting on coming" (and its resultant releasement, or *Gelassenheit*.) It is only through the attuned thinking (and waiting) on the unnecessary that what is to come, can come. Life, from an early stage, teaches us to ignore and to wall off the unnecessary; it teaches us to privilege the necessary instead. Whether it is through education or learned experience, the unnecessary is elided too often by the quantifiable existence of bare life. To the Younger Man, "the burning pain is that we are not permitted to be there [*da sein*] for the unnecessary," the Older Man, warning against ignoring the unnecessary, says, "it is not that the unnecessary is in a state of abandonment, but rather that we — we who do not pay attention to the unnecessary as that which is a necessity — are those who are abandoned."[13] The necessity of the unnecessary is, to the prisoners, like a sound which "even if it should fade away unheard — requires the instrument which gives it off." The unnecessary — even neglected and often damaged — gives life — *vita* — to the denuded existence of the everyday.

A traditional formulation of the necessary can, in itself, be seen dialectically. There is a necessary, so therefore, there must be an unnecessary; if there is something, there must be nothing, for a thing to be there must also be a (no)thing. This is the basis of traditional Western thinking, beginning with Aristotle and the concept of the excluded middle. It is the basis of a logic and a thinking which is scientific and rational, and, at a bare minimum, is all that is necessary to explain to us the world, or at least, a world. Heidegger's two prisoners, in contrast to the above, point us to conceptual thinking that requires something else, a thinking that orients us in a direction that does not lie

---

12 Heidegger, *Country Path Conversations,* 156.
13 Ibid., 155

between two poles of thought (that there is or that there is not), but that, as Jean-Luc Nancy has written, *creates* a world that "is never still" and always "perpetually reopened."[14] The possibility that Heidegger directs us towards is inconceivable, though not, perhaps, inexperienceable, and it is the experience of this inconceivable to which Heidegger orients us in his conceptual thinking on *Ereignis* — the event of being — and *Gelassenheit* — or releasement.

At the end of the telling of the story of Chuang Tzu, the Younger Man says that we should "think of what poetically condenses." This is vague and difficult, at first glance, to apprehend; Heidegger remains elusive and refuses, perhaps, the necessary definitions that one is tempted to place on his words, but this only serves to underline the poetically condensed necessary unnecessary that the prisoners are calling for, and which the Older Man urges the Younger to teach: "Thus, we must learn to know the necessity of the unnecessary and, as learners, teach it to the peoples." The Younger Man replies that "the need and the necessity of the unnecessary […] may perhaps be the sole content of [our] teaching" for years to come.[15]

In a later work, "What Calls for Thinking," Heidegger declares that true thinking is necessarily unscientific, and that science itself famously does not think. For Heidegger, thinking is a leap into the abyssal unknown, into the lacunal space between. In "What Calls for Thinking," Heidegger writes that "there is no bridge here — only the leap," and further, that "we must let ourselves be admitted into questions that seek what no inventiveness can find."[16] To do this, we must "let" ourselves unlearn what we have learned, to let go of scientific knowledge, of what is known on the knowable materialist plane and fall into the "draft" of that which withdraws from us, to make way for a thinking that always pulls away, that always denies interpretation in place of

---

14   Jean-Luc Nancy and Phillipe Lacoue-Labarthe, *Retreating the Political,* ed. Simon Sparks (London: Routledge, 1997).

15   Heidegger, *Country Path Conversations,* 155.

16   Heidegger, *Basic Writings,* 374.

a more originary event, the event of being-thinking. Authentic thinking, for Heidegger, is a pointing towards (what has withdrawn), and therefore, humankind's essential being is a pointer and a sign, but as a sign "remains without interpretation." Authentic thinking for Heidegger allows for the unnecessary to appear as the necessary. It is allows re-orientation towards the ambiguous, rather than remaining in the known. It allows to be *unnamed*, rather than to be *named*.

A concern in this study is to examine what we speak about when we speak. How are we to speak, ontologically (or otherwise), of (a) something (being) which continually pulls away, something that has already necessarily withdrawn, and that only by bearing witness (acknowledging, allowing through releasing) to its withdrawal comes forth? To speak would be to interpret it, to name it and call it forth. This naming would be a challenging, a holding in reserve of the thing, and yet, we must wait in order to allow for a letting come. Naming isolates and separates; (a)waiting is an allowing to come forward. (A)waiting makes the space — clears a clearing — for the emergency of being becoming, for the event of *alētheia*. Using Heidegger as a guide (as a pointer and a sign) towards that which withdraws will be our only way forward, and yet here, too, Heidegger warns us away from using — or saying — a language that "is ever more widely misused and destroyed by incessant talking."[17] In *Contributions to Philosophy (Of the Event)*, Heidegger writes that a language of beings can never reveal truth directly, and even the invention of a new language is impossible. It is only through "transformed saying" that "domains [which] are still closed off to us" can be pushed into. "Thus," writes Heidegger in *Contributions*, "only one thing counts: to say the most nobly formed language in its simplicity and essential force, to say the languages of beings as the language of be-ing."

The play between East and West continues in *A Dialogue on Language*. Written nearly two decades after *Country Path Conversations*, Heidegger continues to explore this saying *that is not*

---

17 Heidegger, *Contributions to Philosophy (Of the Event)*, 54.

a saying. This time, rather than prisoners, Heidegger's dialogue takes places between "an inquirer" (Heidegger) and "a Japanese." The dialogue is a fictionalized account of a meeting Heidegger had with Tezuka Tomio in 1954, and picks up on a conversation on aesthetics that Heidegger had begun with Count Shuzo Kuki in the 1920s. That this "Japanese" is engaged in a questioning with Heidegger is not insignificant, given the difficulty of what they are attempting to talk about. At the start of the text, Tezuka invokes Count Shuzo Kuki and Kuki's teacher Nishida, the primary thinker identified with the Kyoto School, a group of philosophers associated with Kyoto University, which flourished both before and after World War II.[18] It is at this point where the leap (*for there is no bridge*) between Western philosophical thinking and the East becomes most apparent (*comes to be*). Though it is true that Heidegger argues from a place of being, and Eastern philosophical thinking originates from a place of nothingness (*mu*), the two seem to point towards, especially in Heidegger's late thinking, an in-between, a being, or *be*-coming, of no-thing. Nishida's student, Keiji Nishitani, takes up this question of no thing in his *Religion and Nothingness,* a text we will explore more fully in a later chapter. For Nishitani, the concept of relative nothingness, so threatening in a Western context as nihilism, is, when radicalized in Eastern thought as Absolute Emptiness, or the "emptiness of emptiness" (*kūkyo*), becomes a point of practice through which we can (re)assume a radical authenticity, or presentness.

In Heidegger's *Dialogue,* the "Japanese" and his interlocutor attempt to understand a single Japanese word: *iki,* which normally refers to aesthetics, but which the "Japanese,"[19] claims Heidegger, describes as "the pure delight of the beckoning

---

18 Like Heidegger's political past, the history of the Kyoto School is one of a series of mistakes as the thinkers associated with the school found themselves deeply drawn into the political and nationalistic issues of the Imperial Government in the lead up to Japan's imperial expansion and World War II.

19 Here, we cannot be sure if Heidegger is referring to Tezuka Tomio, Count Shuzo Kuki, or using "Japanese" as a collective noun.

stillness."[20] So, like the younger man and the older man who call forth the "pure waiting [that] would be like the echo of pure coming,"[21] so *iki,* to Heidegger, explains the delight of no thing. For Heidegger, again in the words of the "Japanese," *iki,* or that "pure delight" as "the breath of stillness that makes this beckoning delight come into its own is the reign under which that delight is made to come."[22] In response to this, the interlocutor attempts to use *iki* to explain *koto ba,* or language. The "Japanese" translates *koto ba* as "the happening of the lightening message of the graciousness that brings forth [and which holds] sway over that which needs the shelter of all that flourishes and flowers." Heidegger claims that this "wondrous" word which "names something other than our names, understood, metaphysically, present to us: language, glossa, lingua, langue." Heidegger states that this *koto ba* "brings forth" a more fitting word for language, which is "saying" and which "let[s] appear and let[s] shine, but in the manner of hinting." Thinking then, is, through a saying which is not a name for "human speaking," but which "hints and beckons...and is like a saga."

Dōgen's Penetrating Exhaustively

Allowing for something to hint and beckon — to come to be — is not a concern for Eihei Dōgen, the 12th-century Japanese Buddhist thinker, however. Though of an obviously radically different era and culture than Heidegger's, and Nishitani's, many of Dōgen's concerns are similar, and will prove useful (at least in this study) in clarifying some of Heidegger's ideas (and vice versa).

In contrast to a traditional Western concept of things coming to be, things, for Dōgen, already are, and, in being already, the world is "penetrated exhaustively"; the world already is, and

---

20 Martin Heidegger, *On the Way to Language,* trans. Joan Stambaugh (New York: HarperCollins, 1971), 47.

21 Heidegger, *Country Path Conversations,* 147.

22 Heidegger, *On the Way to Language,* 45.

doesn't *come to be*. Our perception of the world remains on the surface; we imagine things to be or not to be, we imagine death and birth to be separate occurrences, absence and presence to occur in relation and against one another. For Dōgen, these things are always already occurring (though not *be*-coming). Being happens not along a teleological path, but as occurrence. Drawing heavily on a concept of time that is the eternal now, or *nikon,* and more importantly on a sort of *timelessness(time)* — a time which occurs without (outside of) time — things in this world simply are. An object, to Dōgen, is its own "independent" being only in the time that it is in right now. This coming to be of an object is a form of stepping back or letting be, of "allowing" something (being or object) to be the object or being that it is at that moment, and not enframing it in what it was, or what it might become. Timelessness(time) does enframe the object, the thing, but only in its own moment (a moment which is not a moment in time, but instead a presencing, an occurring of being-now) as both worthy of that specific time, and as a recognition that there is literally no other time than the time of just now. This acts in exact opposition to the traditional Western metaphysical view of time which sees a series of seriatic, discrete moments stretching forwards and backwards as they pass through the rigid, inevitable portal of the now of present time. Time in the West frames and denotes, capturing objects in order to hold them at bay (in reserve), mining and forming them, making them into something other than what they are in their authentic, primordial self. This ordering or enframing for Heidegger "drives out every other possibility of revealing."[23] For Dōgen, a thing may have a past and a future, but there is no "becoming" of something; things just are already (as they have always already been) in an event of timelessness(time). It is not a "revealing" that takes place so much as a deep recognition that things already are as they are.

In the prosaic Western view, a thing becomes something for us, or at least in relation to us, based on the conceptualization

---

23 Heidegger, *Basic Writings,* 332.

and objectification of the relationship between us and things, or things and other things. A building is there to serve a purpose, as a church or bank or home, as is an ice cream cone, enjoyed, bartered, imagined, as am I. A thing in the world perdures until it no longer does. There is, in this telling, a *telos* to all things and being; being which in its unfolding is temporally located, and centered on a thing's relation to the perceiver. For Descartes, his existence was proven — despite his doubt — through his having thought. For Berkeley, the perceiving of the thing gives it its beingness, its essence. Either way, being remains a subject in an objectified world; things are, and around them lies a world of objects as *res extensa*.

For Dōgen, however, things just are in the time that they are in. This is the essence of the world in the timelessness(time) that is every moment of the absolute now (*nikon*). In his fascicle "Genjōkōan," Dōgen writes:

> Once firewood turns to ash, the ash cannot revert to being firewood. But you should not take the view that it is ashes afterward and firewood before. You should realize that although firewood is at the dharma-stage of firewood, and that this is possessed of before and after, the firewood is at this time independent, completely cut off from before, completely cut off from after. Ashes are in the dharma-stage of ashes, which also has a before and after.[24]

While causally there needs to have been firewood to make ash (and Dōgen, importantly, does not deny this) the actual ash — right now — is just ash; it is not ash that will be used to make lye to make soap, nor is it ash that was once a tree that was once in a forest and that was once an acorn. All these things may have been, but, to Dōgen, in the absolute now (*nikon*) it is just ash, as firewood is just firewood in its own moment, and I am just I, just being, not becoming, not on the road to something.

---

24 Eihei Dōgen, *The Heart of Dōgen's Shōbbōgenzō,* trans. Norman Waddell and Masao Abe (Albany: State University of New York Press, 2002), 42.

Dōgen denies the primacy of causality, emphasizing instead the immediacy of the immediate now. Things are in the moment they are, and not in some undetermined future or already determined past. *This is, but only now.*

This study is not a study in comparative philosophy. It will not attempt to create a synthesis between the ideas of Martin Heidegger and Eihei Dōgen through Keiji Nishitani, nor will it attempt somehow to map those ideas onto the thinkers who follow (in this case I write in the long shadows of Jacques Derrida, Maurice Blanchot, and Jean-Luc Nancy, as well as several thinkers associated with the Kyoto School). This essay instead intends to examine certain key ontological and phenomenological questions concerning being in time, as well as to attempt to read, with Dōgen and Heidegger, how one experiences being itself. It takes up the question which is the question of all questions, and which is never very far from Heidegger — *why is there something instead of nothing?* In this, I will expand the possibly narrow concept of being as being-only-human to include a being of all things, from the paper cup thrown away by a child at a county fair, to the fair itself, the environment, the sky, the earth, the Ferris wheel and, of course, also, but not exclusively the "beings" inhabiting the fair. This study will be an attempt to argue both the "autonomy" of objects (both beings as traditionally conceived and the beingness of a rock, of a mountain, of an ecosphere) and the essential interpenetration of all objects in all things. I will examine these possibilities not from the position of subject, with the world laid out in array, separate but accessible, but from within object-hood itself. Things find both their autonomy and their interpenetration outside of a time of causal relations (past to present, now to then) and in the lacunal present of a timelessness(time), which, for Eihei Dōgen, as for Martin Heidegger, I will posit, are deeply similar, though encompassing important differences.

While Heideggerian concepts will never be enough to explain Dōgen's ideas, nor will Dōgen suffice to explain completely Heidegger, there are corollaries — affinities — and, importantly, echoes of each in the other's thinking. Dōgen's writing on *uji,* or being-time, seems to echo (and to be again echoed by) Heidegger's terms for *Ereignis* and *Gelassenheit*. (N.B. The echo here is not unilateral, omnipotent, univocal — the voice of G-d — but always multivocal, omnidirectional, always repetitive, always already heard, again). In *uji*, according to Dōgen, "we set the self out in array and make the whole world as so many times (*uji*). We must see all the various things of the whole world as so many times (*uji*)." This setting out of the self is done through sustained exertion (*gyoji*), and in doing so "allows" for the whole world to "presence" itself there in that site or clearing where a setting out can occur. This presencing is similar in scope, as I posit, to the event of *Ereignis,* of being becoming, or appropriating itself, to Being. In setting the self out, the "draft" of thinking's withdrawal turns being into being-a-pointer towards that which withdraws. According to Heidegger, "man is the pointer" toward that which withdraws. Withdrawal, for Heidegger, is "an event" and the event of this withdrawal "may even concern and claim man more essentially than anything present that strikes and touches him."[25] This is not to say that the event of *Ereignis* is the same as the event(s) of *uji,* but that one can inform the other. When we attune ourselves to echoes — to the corollaries between the two thinkings — we may better understand the one.

The object of this essay is not to find a synergy between the East and the West, but to use the available tools of a thinking which is global in scope to analyze a problem in the world, the problem of the world itself. In this I seek to attend to the antiphony of difference, of the other, in divergent traditions; I desire no less than to open up spaces for things to be-come, to attempt to traverse landscapes of thinking, searching for new approaches. It is the echo, then, that we seek, and not so much the source. As an example, we can see in the presencing of the absolute now (*nikon*) of the ash described above an approach which perhaps can only be initiated from the West through Heidegger's concept of *Gelassenheit*. To understand the ash in the now, we must

---

25 Heidegger, *Basic Writings,* 375.

allow (*lassen*) for the ash to be simply present, but we must also allow the ash to allow us into (*einlassen*) its essential presencing.

A key difference between Heidegger and Dōgen (besides the most obvious difference of something versus nothing which we will address later) in thinking this world is that Heidegger (at least initially) finds death as the thing that concerns us as beings (Dasein). For Dōgen, life-and-birth are the same occurrence, and are both a duality and singularity at once. Life-and-death are life and they are death; one cannot be without the other (and even here we split the concept too much). Dōgen imagines the world to be becoming through sustained exertion. Thus the rock becomes itself in an array, much as the empty cup does, in the same way as I do. This setting out, however, does not just happen; like the movement occurring in *Gelassenheit,* like the effort it takes the two prisoners to call forth the unnecessary necessary, sustained exertion (*gyoji*) takes just that — hard effort, or practice. Further, as I will argue, sustained exertion requires space; this manifests both as literal space for Heidegger, as in the opening in the forest in which a lightening (*Lichtung*) can take place, or, for Dōgen, within a space in which to practice, as in the meditation hall (a place in which the presencing of all that is can be realized).

For both thinkers, it seems clear: We must respond to the call of thinking, *if only with more thinking.* We must make our mark, even if our mark is far off, even if it is wrong. The emphasis of this call to thinking is not so much on explication, on logic and rational, pragmatic thought, but on a response, or a series of responses. It is in this same spirit that I have tried to engage these thinkers; the facticity of our finitude is a horrifying thing to imagine, as is the notion that this brief time may be wasted. In this vein, it is the doing of philosophy that should concern us; it is the thinking-beyond, which should absorb us utterly. Meister Eckhart, an influence on both Heidegger and Nishitani, writes, "Whoever has understood this sermon, let it be his. Had no one been there, I would have had to preach to this poor-box." With Eckhart then, we imagine a "sermon" that is precisely unfounded, ungrounded, a sermon open to all, the better to begin

a traverse across disciplines and traditions. And, again, as Heidegger writes in "What Calls for Thinking," "There is no bridge
here — only the leap."[26] This leap, then, is a leap into a thinking
that is at once absolutely necessary (*for we have not yet begun to
think*) and irresponsible (with Derrida we can say we are at the
moment of highest irresponsibility in a deep responsibility).[27]
It is a form of thinking which has no answer, not even a name.
It is as much an activity as a practice of thinking as it is a spatiotemporal particular of thought. It is both geographical (an
open space) and a practical activity as a practice of doing; it requires exertion, a refusal to name which is, in its exact negation
(refusal), a positive letting be (permission) of all that is, or possibly can be.

This letting-be is echoed, finally, by Dōgen, who writes, "Yet
for all that, flowers fall amid our regret and yearning, and hated
weeds grow apace." By releasing ourselves into this present moment, we accept and even relish, being's becomingness, its active
objectless existence. By doing so, we accept our own powerlessness, not in the face of God, or in the face of metaphysics, but
in the face of a physical world's worlding, becomings which are
always becominglessness at the same time. There is a soteriological impetus to accepting our own powerlessness; we *be*-come
when we are no longer what we project.

In the next chapter, this project will look at Heidegger's call
for a "new beginning," and specifically follow his argument towards a new form of thinking, a thinking that emerges in the
wake of philosophy's sudden end. Drawing extensively on certain key essays such as "The End of Philosophy and The Task
of Thinking" from 1964, and "What Calls for Thinking?" from
1951, as well as his strangely intoxicating *Contributions to Philosophy (Of the Event)* written between 1936 and 1938, yet un-
published in his lifetime, this chapter will look at how, according

---

26 Martin Heidegger, *What Is Called Thinking?,* trans. by J. Glenn Gray (New
    York: Harper & Row, 1968), 8.

27 Jacques Derrida and Maurizio Ferraris, *A Taste for the Secret,* trans. Giaco-
    mo Donis (Cambridge: Polity, 2002).

to Heidegger, we must practice a different form of thinking. The thinking proposed here is a radical departure from what philosophy — in Heidegger's view having achieved its limit and become suddenly foreclosed by the rational arts — can any longer do; thinking as scholasticism has become an exercise in which what is to be known has already been plotted, archived, named. The thinking proposed by Heidegger is a return to the essential question of being through the transition to "the other beginning." Heidegger writes, and we will attempt to follow him in this, that "in the transition, thought places in dialogue [...] [the] having-been of being and the extreme to-come truth of Being."[28] We will attempt, throughout, to remain with Heidegger in transition, not to perdure or become static, but always to move, to be in the flow. In the same chapter, we will also take up Heidegger's challenge to thinking differently, contrasting it with Dōgen's conception of thinking, or experiencing, the immediate here-and-now of *nikon,* or timeless time. I will examine the two thinkers to find places in which, through reading one, we more fully understand the other. While neither can be entirely understood through the other, there are places where the difficult enigmas of each can be more fully explicated, or at least experienced, through a deeper understanding of the other.

Having prepared ourselves for thinking, chapter three will examine ontologically the presence of time as it manifests in both Dōgen and Heidegger. This chapter will continue to explore Dōgen's *nikon* as a site for the inter-penetration of being times while also examining Heidegger's alleged "turning" from the facticity of being to the imperative of the event, or *Ereignis,* as it manifests itself in the *Contributions.* This chapter pays especial attention to the fact that we — that one — is always already in time, but that that time itself is precisely a question at play in the thinking of both philosophers. For both thinkers, the event of being occurs *within* time (and almost, for Dōgen, *as* time) and it is via the experience of primordial time as timelessness(time) that being, with Heidegger, comes into being-there. The event

---

28 Heidegger, *Contributions to Philosophy (Of the Event),* 7.

discloses itself as truth or *alētheia* through its presencing of time.

Having looked at the types of thinking that Heidegger's "new beginning" requires, chapter four will attempt to chart the "temporal-spatial playing field" that Heidegger, and it would seem Dōgen, both require. Heidegger uses several words to describe this "place," as both a space for beginning to think and also as a very real place of experiencing the transition. This chapter will read in close detail Heidegger's understanding of Nietzsche's "concept of the eternal recurrence of the same" as it relates to Heidegger's experience of the *Augenblick*, or glance of an eye. We will examine closely Heidegger's four volume lecture on Nietzsche from 1944.

Having allowed ourselves to leap with/in the abyssal new, beginning with Heidegger and Dōgen, we will begin again, thinking not the abyss, but the potent concept of Absolute Nothingness (*mu*) as contrasted to nihilism and explored by Keiji Nishitani of the Kyoto school, a movement deeply influenced by and in communication with Heidegger. Though directly influenced by Mahayana Buddhist thought, primarily the Zen tradition of Dōgen, there is much in the Kyoto School's work to recommend these thinkers to a global discussion of the *be*-coming of things. In this chapter, and using Dōgen as a guide, I seek to understand, through Nishitani, the abyssal between proposed by Heidegger.

Chapter six will investigate and follow the idea of practice as it relates, clearly, to Dōgen and Nishitani, and more obliquely to Heidegger. While Dōgen, of cours,e offers a sustained series of writings on *zazen*, or just sitting, as a practice, there are elements in Heidegger and Nishitani that seem to point us towards the readying of oneself in order to experience the abyssal leap. The concept of thinking as meditation, as a readying for — or towards — will be examined, challenging the notion that there are separate domains of thinking and practice, and that, indeed, thinking is, essentially, a practice in meditation.

Chapter seven, as a concluding chapter, will seek to open up the study as conceived so far. The chapter will examine how these modes of thinking the space in between, of thinking the possibilities of the abyssal opening into which thinking the necessary unnecessary of thinking itself can be freed, and how through freeing them (possibilities) we can re-conceptualize our own relations to the world (*relation with-in the world*). Evoking new writings by Timothy Morton, with references to Nancy, Blanchot, and examining Dōgen's *Mountain and Rivers Sutra,* this chapter will seek to divine a line into the new beginning, the beginning again, that Heidegger insists must be possible. This will involve putting into practice the theory that we have grappled with, imagining a new direction forward.

1

A New Thinking (Towards)

A New Form of Thinking

In order to begin to approach the idea of a new beginning with Heidegger in the history of thinking, we have to acknowledge certain endings. Something new, Heidegger seems to indicate, cannot begin while we continue to harbor and shelter old concepts, concepts which have by now — in the bright light of technology's unparalleled dominance — become antiquated and outmoded and which restrict, to Heidegger, "the possibility from which the thinking of philosophy would have to start."[1] For Heidegger, philosophy has become endlessly enmeshed with the advances of science and an increasing technicalization of the world, and this enmeshment has "foreclosed" the project of philosophy, a project conceived perhaps first in the inchoate imagination of pre-Socraticic thinking. Philosophy, as a discipline, has been appropriated or replaced by the more "rational" disciplines of physics and, in general, the sciences. Physics now claims knowledge of, and provides answers to, the question of being, a "field" traditionally investigated by philosophy as metaphysics. The project then of philosophy — born out of the essential thinking *that there is something rather than nothing* — is

---

1   Martin Heidegger, *Basic Writings*, ed. David Farrell Krell (New York: Harper & Row, 1977), 432.

brought to a sudden and possibly premature end. The wonder and awe that so encaptured Parmenides and Heraclitus has been co-opted by a rational "empirical science," which, whenever humans try to think themselves in the world, establishes them not as authentic individuals capable of an original encounter with truth, but rather "on the basis of and according to the criterion of the scientific discovery of the individual areas of beings." The raw possibility of infinite thought is brought to a sudden, premature end; suddenly enclosed, thought is captured by empirical, logical fact, unquestioned and unquestioning in its dominance.

In one of his last formal essays written in 1965, *The End of Philosophy and the Task of Thinking,* Heidegger describes philosophy as a metaphysics "that thinks beings as a whole [...] with respect to Being." This thinking — which is the only issue for philosophy, and which, since the beginning of philosophy, "has shown itself as the ground (*archē…*)" — has become foreclosed by the advent of science. What the sciences have now taken over "as their own task" are the questions that philosophy, in its history, has traditionally grappled with; "the ontologies of the various regions of beings (nature, history, law, art)."[2] Rather than spheres of wonder and thinking, "the arts [have] become regulated-regulating instruments of information."[3] The radical arguments of ontology, of being, of the wonder(ful) awe of something, have, through technology, been reduced to mere repositories of information — mere gathering places of facts. World becomes constrained by *technē,* and there *for us,* and not beside us, or with us in it. In turn, world becomes a mundane puzzle, able to be solved, contained, answerable (*to us*), something we are always already opposed to, removed from. The task, then, is to think a new beginning, a new relation. This beginning, which, at the risk of sounding supercilious, must begin at a beginning that is always unsurpassable, and that, as Heidegger writes, "must constantly be repeated and must be placed [in]

---

2   Ibid., 435.

3   Ibid., 434.

confrontation"[4] with its own uniqueness. This confrontation with itself is precisely what is lacking in the thinking of what philosophy has become.

The foreclosure of philosophy, however, is not an entirely bad thing; for Heidegger, it represents a completion of the project of philosophy and clears the way for this new beginning, or, in the language of *The End of Philosophy,* a "first possibility." But can we, Heidegger asks, think this new possibility in an authentic, originary way, exposing or opening ourselves to a thinking which is "neither metaphysics nor science?" Here Heidegger refuses, as he so often does, an explicit answer; this thinking, he responds, remains "unassuming" for it is only preparatory, it is not (yet) fixed. An answer to this new possibility, this new beginning, remains elusive and avoids a "founding character." For Heidegger, this thinking, as opposed to so much of its history, is "content with awakening a readiness in man for a possibility whose contour remains obscure, whose coming remains uncertain."[5] But how do we ready ourselves for this preparatory thinking, how do we attune ourselves to the task of thinking (as opposed to falling back on the known, the calculable, the already understood, the safe)?

In order to begin thinking anew, in the wake of the disaster of foreclosed thought, Heidegger would have us leap. Unlike Nietzsche's *Twilight of the Idols,* which is subtitled *How To Philosophize with a Hammer,* and in which an active motion is taken against the idols of modernity, Heidegger has us throwing ourselves into the unknown; rather than an active act, he describes one of almost profound surrender. The effect is the same. Faced with the clearing of a destroyed temple, or a space opened in the forest, we are able, as though for the first time (and perhaps, since Plato's *eidos,* it *is* for the first time) to begin to think in an incipient *en*lightened way, especially if we allow the path

---

4   Martin Heidegger, *Contributions to Philosophy (Of the Event),* trans. Richard Rojcewicz and Daniela Vallega-Neu (Bloomington: Indiana University Press, 2012), 45.

5   Heidegger, *Basic Writings,* 436.

of *die Lichtung,* or the lightening of Heidegger's later writings, to open us to an opening.

Heidegger's thinking — from the early lectures on time and phenomenology through the ontological circular hermeneutics of *Being and Time* and "turning" towards the incipient, preparatory thinking of *Contributions* and later writings — returns us, again and again, to the incredibly simple yet equally elusive question of the idea of being (and beings). His work is not a systematic elucidation (declaration) on what Being is; rather, Heidegger is seeking the "question" rather than an answer. It is worthy of the question to ask whether we can read Heidegger not with the technical sobriety of academics (who over and again try to systematize Heidegger) but with a passional response to the call of the question. It is in this sense that the most interesting work of Maurice Blanchot and Jean-Luc Nancy has been done; when we allow ourselves to open to the possibilities of original thinking, those possibilities possibly can open.

In *What Calls for Thinking,* from a series of lectures delivered during the winter and spring semesters of 1951–52, Heidegger gives us some sense of where he wants his conception of thinking to take us; he is opening thinking towards "questions that seek what no inventiveness can find."[6] This aporetic questioning acknowledges, inevitably, failure. Traditional thinking — the thinking of metaphysics and science — directs us towards answers, towards categorical certainties; traditional thinking claims the conceit of there even being an answer. Heidegger's later works — writings produced after what is normally referred to as the "turn" in Heidegger's thought from thinking — are, in essence, products of the exact opposite of the certainty of scientific, rational thinking; of a moving towards a thinking in which what is known becomes — in knowing it authentically — strikingly unknown, becomes unfamiliar, and what is unknown is *known to be unknown,* at the very least. In effect, Heidegger is urging on the very "withdrawal" of a scientific world that

---

6   Martin Heidegger, *What Is Called Thinking* (New York: Harper & Row, 1968), 9.

clouds our experience of being — of the event of truth in be-coming — in order to facilitate the clearing (*Lichtung*) through which the event of being can take place. This is the least (or the most) that we can do; in a preparation for a new beginning we must accept the known to be unknown *or not yet known.* Like phenomena, knowing — as thinking — must be seen to be in a constant state of withdrawal; the point is not to encapture think-ing, as to do so would be to deny its liquid state, to restrict it, and even to enframe it (*Gestell*). Thinking withdraws and we fall in behind it, pulled along by a "draft." We are caught in "the draft of what draws, attracts us by its withdrawal."[7] In *Thinking,* Hei-degger writes that this movement is "quite different from that of migratory birds." We are not seeking, migrating between known points, but rather surrendering, allowing ourselves as possibili-ties to be drawn along. In thinking, we are not pointing towards a known destination, but rather leaving behind an erroneous as-sumption of the known in order to allow it to remain unknown, or at least undeclared; it is the *possibility of being* that remains the question, not the hypostatized conception of a static reality. This is the creative act of thinking, and in the disastrous rem-nants of scientific and technological thought, it is all we can do to begin, again; *the incipient beginning of thinking the beginning beginning again begins again now.*

But to think what remains unthought or unknown is a dif-ficult, almost impossible task; to remain decisively in a space of radical indecision requires a practice of careful maneuver-ing if we are not to descend into a solipsistic maw. Thinking is not a *non*-philosophy, and yet, for Heidegger, authentic think-ing comes only after philosophy, comes only in the wake of philosophy's suddenly foreclosed project. What is authentically unthought can only begin to be thought after philosophy's end. Thinking, when reduced to the discipline of philosophy and treated as one discipline among many, becomes an ossified and artificial practice, rendered scholastic by its unwilled coopting by the sciences. The sciences, by thinking within rigid disci-

---

7   Ibid.

plines, by thinking within specialized spheres, inevitably omit the very foundations on which they are built; they ignore the ground from which their edifice is built. Philosophy as well, when taken captive by the sciences, according to Heidegger, does not look deeply enough, does not examine the *Urgrund* on which, or from which, it comes to be. The task then of thinking is to think *with* philosophy towards its *beyond* as well. Thinking itself must be unthought in order to free itself. Heidegger writes, in *The End of Philosophy and the Task of Thinking,* that "questioning in this way, we can become aware that something that it is no longer the matter of philosophy to think conceals itself precisely where philosophy has brought its matter to absolute knowledge and to ultimate evidence."[8] That something is concealing itself within and without the project of philosophy — within the draft of philosophy's withdrawal — is precisely the issue for thinking, and it is what thinking must think.

But to think in this open manner within the jostling crowd of things, of appearing phenomena, seems nearly impossible. Things (whether computers, airplanes, mugs of beer, beds, Heidegger's (and Nietzsche's) apocryphal hammer, or larger "things," what Timothy Morton calls hyper-objects, such as geographic formations, glaciers, solar systems, universes, relations, and even time itself) gather around us and are ready-at-hand, and to discuss or think the essence of these myriad things is a difficult task indeed. What appears is generally easily thought and dissimulated; the task of thinking, for Heidegger, is to think that which does not easily appear, that which remains concealed in the miasma of radiating phenomena and thus remains unknown to us, secluded within its active withdrawal. This is the task of thinking — to think the remainder of things, to think the things actively withdrawn. To do this, to bring the concealed to present (*Gegenwart*) itself, we need space, a space which Heidegger writes must be "something open, something free," a space in which the up-to-now-concealed is allowed to come

---

8   Martin Heidegger, *On Time and Being,* trans. Joan Stambaugh (New York: Harper & Row, 1972), 64

forth. "Whenever a present being encounters another present being or even lingers near it [...] there openness already rules, the free region is in play."[9]

Heidegger calls this region many things over the years: a *Lichtung* to describe both a lightening, as well as a "forest clearing", and *Offen* to describe "the open." It is within this clearing that the "brightness" of the present (*Gegenwart*) can illuminate itself, where being can have an authentic encounter with truth. *Brightness plays in the open and strives there with darkness.* The brightness of the concealed suddenly illuminated requires as contrast the darkness of what was once concealed. Only within this clearing can what has been heretofore withdrawn presence itself, come to be, and (en)lighten. (It is important to note that Heidegger only reluctantly allows "light" to be associated with brightness or luminosity; he is at pains to say that "what is light in the sense of being free and open has nothing in common with the adjective 'light' which means 'bright.'"[10] Heidegger points us, in a footnote, to a secondary use of the word, which means, 'to alleviate'; however it seems impossible, as many commentators have already noted, to deny — within a history of the enlightenment — the importance of recognizing that *die Lichtung* is indeed a space of light and air, a space made through the very disclosure of the absence of things.) Heidegger writes that "the clearing is the open region for everything that becomes present and absent." Free openness is, and here he uses a "word of Goethe's," an *Urphänomen,* a primal phenomenon. The primal phenomenon of the cleared region itself sets us to the task of learning and lets "it say something to us." But for Heidegger, it is precisely the clearing itself which, within the history of philosophy, has remained without a question, without interrogation, has remained unthought, except at the very beginning of philosophy. We are to think the presence of the clearing in order to allow what is to be present to come forth indeed. What is allowed to be said, or to come forth, is *alētheia,* or the event, or

---

9   Heidegger, *Basic Writings*, 441.
10 Ibid.

presencing, of truth. As the a-privative of the root word refer-ring to the river Lethe, the river of forgetting, *alētheia* means, as much as truth, a remembering of what has always been there, only hidden, forgotten.

Thinking towards a New Beginning

The incipient nature of thinking towards a new beginning is taken up by Heidegger in the strange *Contributions to Philoso-phy (Of the Event)*. Composed (and the enigmatic quality of the "text" seems as much a fugal composition as a written "text") over the course of two years from 1936 to 1938, *Contributions* was, by its very nature, as provisional as the title implies; even Heidegger seemed unsure of its value, showing the text to only a few people in his lifetime (*Contributions* was only published posthumously in German in 1989). And yet it seems, despite its provisionality, there is a profound, if often unrecognized, neces-sity to the project of the *Contributions,* and indeed, within its pages there can be seen the foundations of a new groundwork being laid for Heidegger's later works, even if this ground is pro-visional, not absolute and, importantly, abyssal.

If *Contributions* could be said to be written for someone, or for something, Heidegger writes, it would be for "the few" who "from time to time *question* again," and it would be for "the rare," those who have the strength and "courage" for "solitude," those able to "think the nobility of Being and to speak of its uniqueness."[11] To undertake this challenge towards solitude that questioning requires, we have to first look to Heidegger's own words as a guide; in these words he, again and again, *refuses* the responsibility to say the absolute, to *declare* as such. Com-pared to the vital world-systems of Hegel's *Weltanschauung* or the systematic philosophies of the Anglo-American academy, Heidegger's words are mere utterances, whispered impreca-tions towards a new beginning, but this new beginning resists categorically a definition, or system. It is exactly this concealed

---

11 Heidegger, *Contributions to Philosophy (Of the Event),* 12.

definition which makes Heidegger's work so compelling, and so frustrating. For Heidegger, a "worldview" is a necessarily closed system, and "sets experience on a definite path and within a determinate range, and this in such a broad way that it does not allow the worldview itself to come into question; the worldview thereby narrows and thwarts genuine experience."[12] A worldview already projects its end, and as such "must forgo new possibilities in order to remain one with itself."[13] Philosophy, on the other hand, "is always a beginning" and overcomes itself repeatedly. It is a "terrifying [...] questioning of the truth of Being."[14]

Instead of world-systems, *Contributions* offers ideas *towards* what Heidegger calls a new beginning, not ideas *from* a set of facts. To build *from* is to first acknowledge or accept the premise that there is a solid ground upon which to build an intricate series of causeways and bridges, engineered spans and controlled results; it is to accept that the acquisition of knowledge is teleological or at the very least progressive. To build towards is to not know a direction — it is to actively refuse a direction. It is to not already know, but to imagine, to think towards. We build from solid ground, but we build across the span, into an unknown. To think this way, we must allow ourselves — both in our own thinking (or in a thinking not of a single being but as a people) and in our approach to Heidegger's later writing — to venture into a willing not-knowing that is at once a gamble and irresponsible, even dangerous, but, in contrast to the disaster[15] of modernity, utterly necessary if we are to think beyond our very (at best) limited wor(l)ds.

For Heidegger, "everything would be misinterpreted and would miscarry" if we attempted to provide "an analysis or even a 'definition.'"[16] This stance of radical agnosticism is the neces-

---

12 Ibid., 31.

13 Ibid.

14 Ibid., 30.

15 This is the disaster referred to by Maurice Blanchot in *The Writing of the Disaster,* trans. Ann Smock (Lincoln: University of Nebraska, 1995), 1, in which he writes that the disaster "changes everything."

16 Ibid., 18.

sary "basic disposition" we must assume in order to think "the new beginning." This basic disposition takes a variety of names: "shock, restraint, diffidence, presentiment, foreboding," but each word "merely points to the ungraspableness of everything simple."[17] The shock exists in the literally other-worldly experiencing of the "abyssal in-between" amidst the "'no longer' of the first beginning [...] and the 'not yet' of the fulfillment of the other beginning."[18] How then are we to think within this shocking new beginning that resists analysis and definition?

In the *Contributions*, Heidegger takes up this theme of "the new beginning" explicitly guiding us *forward* and *towards,* though as such he writes that "the issue then is neither to describe nor to explain, neither to promulgate nor to teach."[19] Heidegger offers a chart, a plan towards a "transition to the other beginning" in the form of a "still unmastered ground-plan of the historicality of the transition itself." In order to understand, we must surrender our vulgar, quotidian need for rigid definitions and analysis, to allow ourselves to be swept away, to be, as he writes in "What Calls for Thinking," "caught in the draft of what draws, attracts us by its withdrawal."[20] True thinking for Heidegger "turns away from man."[21] It is in an endless pattern of withdrawal, and "refuses arrival."[22] It can never be formulated into patterned techniques and controlled ideas; but that which withdraws — thinking itself — "may even concern and claim man more essentially than anything present that strikes and touches him."[23] It is always perpetually open, perpetually in a state of movement. This thinking of thinking is radically different from the thinking of the sciences, in which what is known is built upon as solid fact; for Heidegger, science has refused to think the fundamental question of its — and everything's — es-

---

17 Ibid., 19.

18 Ibid., 20.

19 Ibid., 6.

20 Heidegger, *Basic Writings*, 374.

21 Ibid.

22 Ibid.

23 Ibid.

sential ground — *that it is rather than is not.* The "ground-plan" for Heidegger remains "unmastered" and thus still unknown, still undisclosed. Heidegger's call here is as much a practice as it is a system, and though it may be uncomfortable for an academic to accept, to understand it is absolutely necessary to take up Heidegger's ever more insistent call towards a new beginning, to begin to practice *within* the leap.

While we will examine in depth the six steps that Heidegger describes in the Contributions — the *resonating, interplay, leap, grounding, future ones,* and, most difficultly, the *last god* — which will take us "along a way"[24] towards an understanding of being's exposure of itself to Being within the event, it is important that we pause to examine first several of the words already used above; the words "transition," "other [or new] beginning," and "historicality" call us into the place of a temporality (and as such a position of finitude); they place us within time and yet with a future still to come, a future uncertain. The time they place us in, however, is not the time of the vulgar, quotidian day to day time of Aristotle; it is instead a "primordial time," a time that is as unrecognizable to everyday time as the ocean is to a glass of water. Primordial time serves to allow the world of things to presence themselves not as a category à la Kant, but substantially through the evental disclosure of truth. "Transition" is a movement, a passage, a moment of departure (and arrival); it evokes coming-of-age, the passage from one state to another. It speaks to the transit lounge, and to the trepidation of a voyage. But a voyage begins from a known point while Heidegger insists not on a different end, but a different beginning. This beginning is a new

---

24 The title of §1 is rendered by Rojcewicz and Vallega-Neu, in their 2012 translation of the *Beiträge zur Philosophie (Vom Ereignis),* as "These 'contributions' question along a way" (Heidegger, *Contributions to Philosophy (Of the Event),* 6). Parvis Emad and Kenneth Maly render the same sentence, in their 1999 translation of the *Beiträge,* as, "'Contributions to Philosophy' enact the questioning along a pathway" (Martin Heidegger, *Contributions to Philosophy (From Enowning),* trans. Parvis Emad and Kenneth Maly [Bloomington: Indiana University Press, 1999], 3). The German reads, in the Vittorio Klostermann edition from 2003, "Die 'Beitrage' fragen in einer Bahn."

"originary position," a primordial return to an unknown source (though we know the source exists, we cannot know the source), an opening to the givenness of the question. "Historicality" is a technical term for Heidegger which refers us to the existential issue of our own finitude. We are not, according to Heidegger, bounded by a series of eternally occurring nows; rather (and this is one way he differs from Dōgen's existential analysis of temporality) we are defined by a unity "stretched between birth and death," a unit that is historically disclosed and determined. Beings are determined by their historical becoming-present through the disclosures of the event.

Dōgen's "Wide Circular Sea"

While it would be deeply disingenuous to attempt to parlay Dōgen's thinking into something on par with Heidegger's thinking *towards*, it may be possible to pause and examine where Dōgen's thinking leads us, or can lead us, and whether or not there is not something that accurately echoes some of the thinking that Heidegger would have practiced, in both *Contributions* and elsewhere. Our purpose in this study is not to prove that Heidegger is a secret Buddhist, nor that Dōgen is a Heideggerian; rather, our hope is to examine the two side by side, reading one through the other, allowing their thoughts to inter-penetrate each other, *to speak to each other.* While Dōgen's[25] concern is not explicitly with the thinking of thinking nor philosophy, he is evoking a new form of thinking as a way to get to his own particular form of enlightenment. It is a popular mis-conception to simplify Buddhist teaching as mere nihilism towards the denial of Being, which risks a simplification that leads to an erroneous — or deeply constrained — way of thinking, and which denies to Dōgen — and substantial parts of the Buddhist can-

---

25 Dōgen was not always treated as a "philosopher," and it was not until the work of Watsuji Tetsurō (1889–1960) and Tanabe Hajime (1885–1962), both influential thinkers of the Kyoto School, that his ontological and phenomenological import was recognized. Prior to this, the treatment of Dōgen's work was limited primarily to the work of Soto exegetics.

on — the richness and subtlety that this thinking inspires. Like Heidegger, Dōgen rejects systematic answers in favor of leaving "open" the questions of existence to the dynamism of a "leapt" thinking. Both Dōgen and Heidegger, as we have already seen (and will continue to see) direct us towards a thinking that is at once deeply familiar, though endlessly withdrawn, from our inauthentically constrained world.

Dōgen is thought to have written — or included — "Genjōkōan" as either the first or the second fascicle of the *Shōbōgenzō* in mid-autumn of 1233. Though written for a layperson, the highly enigmatic and ambivalent style of "Genjōkōan" leave it open to interpretation and yet it is at times utterly impenetrable. It has been hailed as the core of Dōgen's work, the "skin, flesh, bone, and marrow" of his thinking according to Nishari Bokuzan (and cited by Waddell and Abe[26]) of the Meiji era. The entire *Shōbōgenzō* is variously said to contain 60, 75, 12, or 28 books, though in its entirety, and published as the Honzan edition, it contains ninety fascicles. In two of the collections (the 60-book and the 75-book), "Genjōkōan" leads the collection, while it is dropped from the 12- and 28-book editions, and appears as third in the complete *Honzan* edition. Despite the discrepancy, Dōgen himself is thought to have put together the two larger editions of the fascicles, and thus we see him prioritizing "Genjōkōan" by placing it at the beginning. Though written early in his life, Dōgen is said to have reworked "Genjōkōan" for most of his career, and indeed, according to Steven Heine,[27] the "Genjōkōan" was one of the final pieces that Dōgen undertook, even half a decade after work on the entire *Shōbōgenzō* was completed.

The title "Genjōkōan" is difficult to translate. According to an introduction by Norman Waddell and Masao Abe, *Genjō* literally means "becoming manifest" or "immediately manifesting

---

26 Eihei Dōgen, *The Heart of Dōgen's Shōbōgenzō,* trans. Norman Waddell and Masao Abe (Albany: State University of New York Press, 2002). P.39

27 Steven Heine, ed., *Dōgen: Textual and Historical Studies* (Oxford: Oxford University Press, 2012).

right here and now."[28] Waddell and Abe translate *Genjōkōan* as "Manifesting Suchness," while Steven Heine prefers to title the fascicle "Spontaneous Realization of Zen Enlightenment," and Hee-Jin Kim, another prominent commentator and translator on Dōgen's works, translates it as "The Kōan Realized in Life." For our purposes, we must respect that the *kōan* is an essential aspect of the title, and points towards a manifesting that cannot be understood except to a few (*to the rare*). To Waddell and Abe, and importantly, for us, "immediately manifesting right here and now" does not mean that something not already manifest is suddenly manifested; rather, the *immediate presence* "of all things as they truly are in their suchness, untouched by our conscious strivings"[29] is suddenly made apparent. "Genjōkōan" means, to Dōgen, that all things become apparent in their legitimate (and authentic) *manner*. It is in this sense that we can begin to read back and forth between Heidegger and Dōgen. Truth, or world, or Being, has already appeared; it is our misconceptions and inauthenticities that constrain the event (or *dharma*) to concealment. Clearing the way through practice or leapt thinking has the effect of bringing the concealed and withdrawn to the fore, into the site of disclosure.

As in the evental site in Heidegger's writing, there is a "moment" of clarity in Dōgen — which he will call, in the Zen tradition — *satori,* meaning, in general terms, enlightenment. However, it is critical to note that *satori,* sometimes called *kensho,* is not a one-to-one translation as enlightenment; rather, *satori* is, broadly, a conscious insight into the essential nature of the universe. While exact interpretations of *satori* vary between Buddhistic traditions, for Dōgen, *satori* was not considered to be the pinnacle of practice; rather, *satori* provides a momentary glance into the reality of the world (that it is empty). In this way, *satori* could be seen to work in a similar way to the clearing or opening in Heidegger's thinking of *alētheia*. Like the evental site, *satori*

---

28 Dōgen, *The Heart of Dōgen's Shōbōgenzō,* 40.

29 Norman Waddell and Masao Abe, Introduction to Dōgen, *The Heart of Dōgen's Shōbōgenzō,* 39.

defiantly is not transcendental in that it is not a permanent state, nor does it "transport" one anywhere (at least not permanently); *satori* is instead a transitory state in which reality is perceived as suddenly denuded of our own expectations. Dōgen saw the event of *satori* as not a final, teleological end point of practice, but still as an essential part of it. For Dōgen, true enlightenment involved an integration of one's perception of the world and one's actions within that world. He writes in the "Genjōkōan" that, "acting on and witnessing oneself in the advent of myriad things is enlightenment."

In Dōgen's opening paragraph of "Genjōkōan," he describes a world that is always already in flux, always already in the full throes of becoming, whether we attune ourselves to this world or not. He writes,

> When all things are Buddha Dharma, there is illusion and enlightenment, practice, birth, death, Buddhas, and sentient beings. When all things are without self, there is no illusion or enlightenment, no birth or death, no Buddhas or sentient beings. The Buddha Way is originally beyond any fullness or lack, and for that reason, there is birth and death, illusion and enlightenment, sentient beings and Buddhas. Yet for all that, flowers fall amidst our regret and yearning, and hated weeds grow apace.[30]

In the context of Dōgen's thinking, "Buddha Dharma" refers to what he calls the "samādhi of self-fulfilling activity." This *samādhi* (which can in itself best be described as a position of abiding in, or resting into) signifies a total freedom of self-realization without dualisms or the constraints of dialectical aporetic blockages. It describes a moment of self-realization in which inauthentic notions of an individual, concrete self melt away and one is left immediately present *with*in a world (whereas before one was *with*out a world). This is not simply an abstract principle but rather a practice, or activity, in itself. As we have seen

---

30 Dōgen, *The Heart of Dōgen's Shōbōgenzō,* 40.

with Heidegger's leap (developed later into *Gelassenheit*), there is, in this practice, a profound surrendering of the control we normally exert, with a sometimes manic desperation, in regards to the world around us. This surrender is not, however, drawn from a place of weakness or timidity; it is rather, with Heidegger, the willed leap, and with Dōgen it is total exertion (*gyoji*). What Dōgen directs us towards in the above passage is the position of the practitioner in relation to a world of flux and change, a world of birth and death in which we, on one level, cannot take part. In the first place, when all things are Buddha Dharma, within the world of prosaic, everyday experiences, there are the horrifying dichotomies of birth and death, enlightenment and sentient beings; life is an uncontrolled, unpredictable and chaotic place. Through an initial encounter with Buddha Dharma — with the *samādhi* of self-fulfilling activity which at once destroys and devours inauthentic experiences of self and others — these dichotomies seem to dissolve, only to reappear in the third and final state when these dichotomies — no longer feared or denied — are accepted with an equanimity through an authentic exposure of the selfless self to the inherent emptiness of all *dharma,* or eventing phenomena. Despite our deepest desires to the contrary — in whatever form of wishes, prayers, incantations, manias, and distractions that we choose to manifest them in — flowers fall and hated weeds grow apace; life, in its most primordial and originary form, unfolds as it is, not how we wish it to be.

Following this paragraph, Dōgen describes the world as it *presences* itself to us. He writes that the "practice that confirms things by taking the self to them is illusion: for things to come forward and practice and confirm the self is enlightenment."[31] If we exert our *selves* forward or towards something in an inauthentic way, we remain in delusion (and inaccessible to the ground of truth); if we allow for things to come forward, to allow things to become what they already are, we support things in their authenticity and we allow ourselves to experience truth

---

31 Ibid., 40.

manifesting as such. Dōgen continues: "When they realize one side, the other side is in darkness." That which appears to us on one hand is always enclosed in a darkness on the other. To put it in Heideggerian terms, what comes forward into the clearing is already receding into an ever encroaching darkness. As with Heidegger, we cannot stay in this place for long; the clearing grows dark as does the *en*lightening moment in which we perceive all things as Buddha-dharma. Dōgen continues in the next paragraph:

> To learn the Buddha Way is to learn one's self. To learn one's self is to forget one's self. To forget one's self is to be confirmed by all dharmas. To be confirmed by all dharmas is to cast off one's body and mind and the bodies and minds of others as well. All trace of enlightenment disappears, and this traceless enlightenment continues on without end.[32]

To engage with one's self we must first forget the self, first cast off delusional misunderstandings about a concrete, perduring permanent self, a self which exists in any way separate from others or other phenomena. In recognizing that the self has no inherent perdurance, we rescue that self from a false constraint of the self. In this same way, we cast off ideas of enduring entities of any sort (whether infinite beings or existent selves). Only in this way do we come to be "confirmed" as no-self, and only in this way does enlightenment (which we see as the evental event of truth presencing itself,) or *satori,* occur, becoming, in its very coming to be, traceless, unstained. It is important to note that despite this "traceless enlightenment" continuing without end, Dōgen is not giving enlightenment a special, permanent designation; enlightenment "happens" in a sort of timeless time, what in the West might best be described as a form of primeval, *kairological* time or, with Heidegger, in a primordial, originary

---

32 Ibid., 41.

ECHOES OF NO THING

site which exists beyond or before our prosaic conceptions of *chronological* time.[33]

In "Genjōkōan," Dōgen describes the experience of encountering the *samādhi* of self-fulfilling activity, or Buddha Dharma in nearly *kairotic* terms. The experiences of self-fulfilling activity fills the body and mind, yet we experience lack. He writes,

> It is like boarding a boat and sailing into a broad and shoreless sea. You see nothing as you gaze about you but a wide circle of sea. Yet the great ocean is not circular. It is not square. It has other, inexhaustible virtues. It is like a glittering palace. It is like a necklace of precious jewels. Yet it appears for the moment to the range of your eyes as an encircling sea. It is the same with all things […]. If we are to grasp the true and particular natures of all things, we must know that in addition to apparent circularity or angularity, there are inexhaustibly great virtues in the mountains and seas. We must realize that this inexhaustible store is present not only all around us, it is present right beneath our feet and within a single drop of water.[34]

What we see around us is only what is most apparent. Beneath the phenomena of appearances — the jostling crowd of things coming to be, the "myriad dharmas" — lies an "ocean" of inexhaustibly great virtues of things manifesting which are only hidden from us because of our own lack of insight. In the same fashion, each thing as it comes to be has infinite myriad events coming to be within it (and through it) at every moment. As in Heidegger's evental thinking towards a new beginning, if we think differently, or again, or begin again, we begin *again* to experience a world not yet disclosed to us, but which is already there. Dōgen compares this essential ignorance towards the

---

33 Heidegger uses the term *kairos* to describe a "moment" (*Augenblick*) between past and future, a time which cannot be mapped or defined, but only predicted and anticipated.
34 Dōgen, *The Heart of Dōgen's Shōbōgenzō*, 43.

"ocean" of phenomena, enigmatically, to the environs of a fish, or a bird. A fish is unaware of anything beyond the water; its world is, infinitely, the waters. So it is for the bird whose world is finitely constrained in the air, which it views as infinite. For beings *in their world,* our world seems similarly "known." To begin to think again, to open ourselves to the essential opening of the clearing, as in the practice of *satori,* is to begin again, with what Heidegger calls a new beginning, and Dōgen's Zen tradition a "beginner's mind."

2

The Questioning of All Questions

A Fugal Repetition

In *Contributions,* Heidegger returns to certain themes brought up in *Being and Time. Contributions* takes up, *again,* the questions first thought in the work of the previous decade; the question of being, temporality or finitude, historicality and truth are raised and questioned — *again* — this time in a radical, sustained, and (possibly) even more confusing way than in *Being and Time.*[1] (Declaring it confusing, however, in no way diminishes the work; Heidegger's call *towards* will remain always preparatory, provisional, and, above all, transitional, and thereby already resistant — in its very simplicity — to the formation of a concrete definition.) Following Heidegger's turn in thinking, the triadic appearance of *Contributions, The Event,* and *Mindfulness*[2] seem more honest in their utter rejection of a classical system in which to explore these questions; *Contributions* resists

---

1   There is a place where Heidegger questions his system in *Being and Time.*
2   As already mentioned, *Contributions* was written between 1936–38, and was followed by *Mindfulness* (*Bessinung*), written in 1938–39, and *The Event* (*Das Ereignis*), written in 1942–43. These dates are culled from the Vittorio Klostermann *Gesamtausgabe,* which is still an ongoing effort. Accordingly, each title is part of a collection organized by Klostermann. *Das Ereignis* is also known as the *Gesamtausgabe* 65, *Bessinung* as the *Gesamtausgabe* 66, and *Das Ereignis* as the *Gesamtausgabe* 71.

a clear plan — it is rather a call, a movement (in the originary sense of the word), a leap into the abyssal unknown which is a new beginning. It is a fugal repetition of that initial questioning into being itself and the questioning gives way, passes into, a sounding (*Anklang*), or resonating of the question itself. Heidegger writes,

> In order for this attempt to become an actual impetus, the wonder of questioning must be experienced in carrying it out and must be made effective as an awakening and strengthening of the power to question.[3]

The project of *Contributions,* then, is not to provide an answer, another system; it provides no clear way forward, nor does it provide a concrete analysis of a phenomenon. Rather, Heidegger asks — as he has done since the beginning — that we embrace, or rather open ourselves to, the wonder of the questioning that is a question, that is the question of Being, and the only question finally which is "question-worthy." In order to "awaken" we must experience first that wonder (which, as we shall see, could be related — *provisionally, transitionally* — to the beginner's mind of Zen practice, or to the doubting of Nishitani.) In §4 of *Contributions,* Heidegger writes that, though questioning at times risks "amounting to an empty, obstinate attachment to the uncertain, undecided, and undecidable," and could seem to simply be a "backtracking of 'knowledge' into idle meditation,"[4] we must do so. For, as he continues,

> in questioning reside the tempestuous advance that says "yes" to what has not been mastered, and the broadening out into ponderable, yet unexplored, realms. What reigns here is a self-surpassing into something above ourselves. To ques-

---

3   Martin Heidegger, *Contributions to Philosophy (Of the Event),* trans. Richard Rojcewicz and Daniela Vallega-Neu (Bloomington: Indiana University Press, 2012), 10.

4   Ibid.

tion is to be liberated for what, while remaining concealed, is compelling.[5]

To say "yes" is to exist within the future of possibilities; it is an ecstatic stance that opens rather than closes; it is to accept the unknown with equanimity, with care. The "yes" compels being into an authentic experience with Being, away from the quotidian, everyday experience of mundane reality.

To those who are not, or cannot be, "compelled" by this radical questioning (which is, in itself, an extension of Descartes' radical doubt, though Heidegger does not stop within the certainty of the *cogito* but rather insists on us going far beyond), Heidegger seems to have little to say. They "do not belong in the invisible ring enclosing those whose questioning is answered by the intimation of Being"[6]; indeed, to those who exist solely within this mundane age of "infinite wants stemming from the concealed plight of a lack of a sense of plight," writes Heidegger, "this question must necessarily seem the most useless idle talk."[7] Heidegger's gesture is one towards an aristocracy of thinking, to the, as already mentioned above, *the rare, the few*.

This questioning of the few cannot be a mere rethinking of what has come before, using the same language; Heidegger instead points us towards thinking the beginning of a new "beginning of another history."[8] As unavoidable as is the confrontation with the first beginning of the history of thought, just as certainly must questioning itself forget everything with which it surrounds itself, and merely think its own plight.[9]

This question is, resolutely, "the question of all questions."[10] For Heidegger, everything is at stake in the act of questioning; it is not simply an intellectual exercise. The question can only be,

---

5   Ibid.
6   Ibid., 11.
7   Ibid.
8   Ibid.
9   Ibid.
10 Ibid.

for Heidegger, the "retrieval of beings out of the truth of Being."[11] We must become thinkers as questioners, in order that the "the truth of being, the grounding of Da-sein, becomes necessary" *again*.[12] This cannot be a mere systematic understanding or processing; it must be, for Heidegger, as he writes in *Contributions* and elsewhere, not a bridge but a leap, "the leap carried out by the human being as the seeker of Being, i.e., as the *thinker* who creates."[13] Thinking this way, then, is a profoundly creative act in which one exposes oneself *to the question, to the unknown*. To fall, one does not need a system; one needs only the will, the will to question, to think, to surrender. It is as though Heidegger is attempting to clear the ground in an act not dissimilar to Nietzsche's "philosophy with a hammer," directing us to, not to smash idols, but to think differently, in a radically new way; the effect, however, is the same — radical, unsurpassed change. "The questioners have broken the habit of curiosity; their seeking loves the abyss, in which they know the oldest ground."[14] This movement towards a "new beginning" is a transition out of traditional metaphysical thinking (whereby Being is singular, infinite, and all-encompassing) to another, very different way of thinking. It is an opening of one's being to the possibility that the ground on which we have based our thinking is no longer there, that there is another ground, older, more primordial, more basic which until now we have not even considered, a ground which Heidegger calls the abyssal ground (*Abgrund*).

How are we to think ourselves without a metaphysical ground, a ground which until this point had been the only ground there was? This is the beginning of thinking a new beginning, and of no longer separating Being and beings as if they were divisible, objectifiable, hypostatized entities. Through the leap towards a new beginning, we manage to join Being and be-

---

11 Ibid.
12 Ibid., 24.
13 Ibid., 11.
14 Ibid., 13.

ings, thinking the new beginning as an authentic event without the entrapments of a metaphysical history.

Like Dōgen, whose rhetoric illustrates opposites and describes everyday, seeming dualities, while all the while destroying them as false and delusional, Heidegger never denies that they continue to exist. That they occur as a reality (but never compromise an *entire reality*) means only that these dichotomies manifest on a single, obvious plane of the everyday. Through careful examination of ground, or by attending to one's situation with a clear, precise mind, we can begin to see that all phenomena are, with Heidegger, groundless, and with Dōgen, empty of inherent essence. Dōgen writes that when a person "practices and realizes the Buddha Way," when they have attuned themselves and when "they have attained one dharma, [they] penetrate it exhaustively; when [they] encounter one practice, [they] practice that one practice."[15] When, through whatever practice or thinking, we enter into an authentic encounter with the event of truth — be it through the sudden enlightenment of Zen *satori* or through the immediate, transformative "site of the moment" (*Augenblicksstätte*) of Heidegger's *Contributions* — the world of opposing antinomies begins to break down in this new abyssal, fluctuating, and fluid beginning *beginning again*.

The Falling Silent of Deep Listening

We are in the abyss without the comforting ground of a metaphysical presence or answer (we are beings without ground) and this, in effect, opens our being, according to Heidegger, to a radical shock (*Erschrecken*). Thinking as ordinarily practiced in the quotidian world shelters us, and allows us not to think "what is most worthy of the question."[16] It inures us from thinking the most primordial, basic questions and as such we remain out of touch and removed from what is most important to us. It is only,

---

15 Eihei Dōgen, *The Heart of Dōgen's Shōbōgenzō,* trans. Norman Waddell and Masao Abe (Albany: State University of New York Press, 2002), 44.

16 Heidegger, *Contributions to Philosophy (Of the Event),* 11.

according to Heidegger, the effect of shock which can shatter us — our systems of knowledge, our way of being — and rescue us from the ordinary, from the easily answerable. But in doing so, shock propels and springs us into a new place of "openness" from which what is most unknown and most unthought — for Heidegger, *the abandonment and withdrawal of being from beings* — can begin to be thought, as though for the first time — as a *new beginning.* The shock of thinking this way does not cause us — *the few, the rare* — to withdraw, though it could; rather it presages a radical transition away from the false grounding of traditional metaphysical thinking of one in the world, and towards creatively thinking the possibility of being as authentic, historical being. This shock opens "the self concealing of Being," which in turn is joined by its own "will" which Heidegger calls "reticence" (*Verhaltenheit*),[17] or "the creative withstanding [*Aushalten*] in the abyss."[18]

It is in this creative withstanding through reticence and restraint, and through the practice of an ennobled silence (falling silent to the old questions, the questions of metaphysics and world systems), that the clamor of Being's withdrawal from beings is heard. Falling silent avails to us the abyssal possibility of the new beginning, but this silence is in no way is a quiescence as in a form of surrender; rather, it becomes an emboldened stance *towards* not a force *against*; reticence and restraint (as silence) look into and across the abyss. There is a "hesitant self-withholding" in reticence, a self-withholding that allows for what is to come, *to come,* to emerge. This is perhaps best illustrated in language; in dialogue, if we "withhold" our words, we "allow" for our interlocutor to say what they mean to say. What is to be revealed is revealed in the gaps between, in the silences that happen between thoughts. In reticence, we hold back our vulgar assertion to being — our clamorous insistence — and we

---

17 *Verhaltenheit* is translated as "restraint" by Rojcewicz et al. but Emad and Maly in their 1999 translation of the *Beiträge* as "reticence." Considering the focus on silence, solitude and stillness, it seems better to stay with Emad's translation, following the latin *re-tacere,* to be silent.

18 Heidegger, *Contributions to Philosophy (Of the Event)*, 30.

thereby "allow" for Being to emerge. This emergency takes place as event in which being comes into its own, to an authentic, emboldened state.

Falling silent attunes us first to a listening (to a deep stillness) rather than a saying (of a cacophony). Falling silent and stillness are deeply interpenetrated, and Heidegger writes that "this stillness arises only out of keeping silent. And this bringing into silence grows only out of reticence [*Verhaltenheit*]."[19] In our hesitancy, in our holding back, our withholding, we transition from the clamor of individual being asserting itself and enter into what Heidegger characterizes as meditative awareness, or, more simply, meditation (*Besinnung*), the attunement to a new beginning. Heidegger's meditation is not just a meditation on oneself, but serves the process within inceptual thinking, of moving oneself to a new concern of selfhood.

> The meditation of inceptual thinking concerns us (ourselves) and yet it does not. It does not concern us so as to bring out from us the prescriptive determinations; but it does concern us as historical beings and concerns us specifically in the plight of the abandonment of beings (at first, decline in the understanding of being, and then forgetting of being). It concerns us, who thus are initially posited in our exposure amid beings; it concerns us in this manner in order that we find our way beyond ourselves to selfhood.[20]

We are beginning to think the new beginning, we are beginning to think what is *most question-worthy,* and this most question-worthy of questions takes us from the petty concerns of everyday existence — concerns about money and love and hunger — towards the concerns of a larger, more primordial, more incipient nature, a nature not yet thought. In this, Heidegger goes far further than he has in the past. He writes that it is tempting to dismiss the entire thinking of *Being and Time* as "limited

---

19 Ibid., 29, translated amended.
20 Ibid., 55.

to the sphere of an anthropology."[21] The concerns in *Contributions* point us towards fundamental existential problems that are, in effect, larger than the mere mortal — though messianic they continue to resist metaphysics — and it is this preparation towards an inceptual thinking that has begun to make the way ready for a new opening, a new beginning, one that will lead, in Heidegger's words, to

> the opening of the simplicity and greatness of beings and the originally compelled necessity of securing in being of securing in beings the truth of Being so as to give the historical human being a goal once again, namely, to become the one who grounds and preserves the truth of Being, to be the "there" as the ground required by the very essence of Being, or, in other words, to care.[22]

It is only through this new conception of a language without metaphysical constraints or conceits, in the clearing and lightening (*Lichtung*) of the openness of being to the possibility of Being that the historical human being has a role again, has a purpose, and this purpose, unanswered but obvious, is towards becoming, through *care,* being essential being.

That is what care means, neither a trivial fussing over just anything, nor a renunciation of joy and power, but something more original than all that, because care is uniquely "for the sake of Being" — not of the Being of the human being but the Being of beings as a whole.[23]

Inceptual thinking has carried us from the new beginning to a new being (amongst Being). It is the formulation of care, or concern, that explodes the human being from an individual concerned with itself to a being that is concerned with the "whole."

---

21 Ibid.
22 Ibid., 15.
23 Ibid.

3

The Question of Time

The Question(s) of Time(s)

In our discussion of a new beginning, and the inception of thinking, we have scarcely dwelled (*begun to dwell*) on one very important aspect that represents Heidegger's challenge (to us and
to himself — *to the rare*), as well as to his "turning" of his thinking in the mid-1930s from the facticity of being to the imperative
of the event, or *Ereignis*. The question of time has so far been
barely investigated, but as a concept looms large for the thinker;
the event of being occurs within time (and almost, with Dōgen,
as time), and it is through the disclosure of a primordial time
that being *be*-comes being-there, or Dasein. Heidegger's work
is as much a practice of thinking differently from the tradition
of philosophy, as it is a philosophical encounter with the idea
of being-there (and with the time of being-there), and as such
we must leave open the way for this new beginning (of *incipient
thinking*) to make its own disclosure apparent to us. In this we
require an attunement and resoluteness in the practice of attain-
ing radical openness. Critically, this is not a quietude towards
which Heidegger directs us, but rather a practice of profound
acceptance, a falling into the slipstream of the draft. The surren-

der into the leap, the letting go or releasement (*Gellasenheit*),[1] the abiding in and dwelling, the anticipatory resoluteness of the being toward death; all of these begin to call us towards an acceptance of a world that remains at once very close and impossibly remote, a world uncontrollable, though not uncontrolled, possibly predictable, albeit not to us.

This uncontrollable world is a concern for Dōgen as well, though, like Heidegger, Dōgen counsels a "standing by" within the uncontrolled chaos of time (rather than trying to contain and manipulate it.) His philosophy is clearly one of meditation (his primary teaching is of *shiken-taza*, or *zazen*-only, which, as we will see in more detail below, directs one to just "sit," actively, within the world). In his fascicle "Uji," also a part of the *Shōbōgenzō*, Dōgen writes, that, in manifesting oneself within a world, "you must not by your own maneuvering make it into nothingness; you must not force it into being."[2] In a way similar to what we have seen in Heidegger, world worlding must not be interfered with in Dōgen. Indeed, to take an action is in effect to restrict, and create an inauthentic, artificial world; however Dōgen, like Heidegger, does not interpret this as a form of quietism. Rather, this standing in is an active being-there (Dasein) of being-time (*uji*).

For Heidegger, time — like the idea of being, like the idea of thinking itself — needs to be rethought, re-apprehended, in order to "allow" for the presencing of truth as *alētheia*, or in the event of *Ereignis* making itself manifest through its own disclosure. This requires a different and difficult approach to the question of time itself if we are to understand it (and, as we shall see, one which is fluid and self-surpassing as we move from the years before *Being and Time* to the years following *Contributions*).

---

1   Heidegger rarely used this term prior to his "turning" and never with the specificity that it came to mean prior to the end of the war when *Gelassenheit* — specifically the letting go or releasement of being into Being began to be used with formal intention.

2   Eihei Dōgen, *The Heart of Dōgen's Shōbōgenzō*, trans. Norman Waddell and Masao Abe (Albany: State University of New York Press, 2002), 53.

In *Being and Time,* Heidegger works to counter common "everyday" notions of time, notions inherited from Aristotle (and which extend through to Bergson), as well as a history of a metaphysical thinking that grants permanency to a supreme Being but which constricts an understanding of time to a series of ever-reproducing "now-points" located in a continuum stretching between past and present. Time is seen as a fact, and its progression is predictable and dependable. In Aristotle's *Physics,* he writes that "It is clear […] that time is 'number of movement in respect of the before and after,' and it is continuous since it is an attribute of what is continuous."[3] These "now-points" stand in relation to that continuum, Aristotle explains, as a point stands in relation to a line; the point is not a part of that line but marks, as a separate phenomenon, a place on that line "that both connects and terminates […]. It is the beginning of one and the end of another."[4] However this is treated, time remains a constant, inescapable other within the continuum. For Heidegger, however, time is apprehended in two ways; initially, and in the everyday, it is taken as a vulgar measurement through which, as Aristotle distinguishes it, time exists between things and is measured, adduced, plotted. In the second way, Heidegger sees the existence of another, deeper, more originary, and primordial temporality through which Dasein, or being-there, becomes, or appropriates, its authentic self. It is with this primordial temporality and the echoes we hear in Dōgen, which we will be focused on in this chapter.

Eihei Dōgen also approaches time "differently" than how we "normally" experience it. For Dōgen, we "should not come to see that time is *only* flying past" or as "something that *goes* past."[5] Rather, time presences itself not as a series of past and present times that "overlap or pile up in a row," but in a form, to Dōgen, not unlike "spring […] with all of its many and varied

---

3   Aristotle, *Physics,* Book IV, 11.
4   Ibid.
5   Dōgen, *The Heart of Dōgen's Shōbōgenzō,* 51.

signs."[6] Time, for Dōgen, on the one hand, is a series of inter-
locked nows, but, more importantly, these "nows" are interpenetrated "being-times dwelling." The result is that, literally, everything is "being-time"; as in Heidegger's temporality, everything
that is, is already time. Time becomes the primordial ground
through which things are, or come to be. This can be contrasted
with Kant's ontological categories of time and space, in that time
is not something through which we experience a world; time is,
so everything else is, too. Rather than seeing time as a separate
entity, something through which phenomena pass, for Dōgen,
time is, as everything else is; it is not limited to a mere continuum nor is it anything which can be removed from things in
the world, nor from world itself. Dōgen writes that "mountains
are time, and seas are time. If they were not time, there would be
no mountains and sea."[7] Time here acts predictably perhaps as a
logos, presupposing and allowing for the presence of phenomena within its field, but time *is* also, as other things are. Without
time, "things would be not-so."[8] We will attempt to address these
concepts in greater detail below, as well as where they help (or
hinder) our understanding of Heidegger.

The Time of Being and Time

Heidegger's first published attempts towards thinking *Sein* (being) and *Zeit* (time) differently came after nearly twelve years
of silence in which he published nothing. This was a time during which, though he was teaching extensively (and many of his
lectures from that period are now "texts") he brought onto final
being nothing. *Being and Time* then came as a sudden shock to
the philosophic community. According to Theodore Keisel's *The
Genesis of Being and Time,* Heidegger attempted three different
drafts before the final; these are known as "The Dilthey Draft:
The Concept of Time," "The Ontoneroteric Draft: History of the

---

6   Ibid., 54.

7   Ibid., 56.

8   Ibid.

Concept of Time," and the "The Final Draft: Toward a Kairology of Being." It is important to note that each of the titles of these drafts, as does the book in its final form, contains an allusion to time, while only two acknowledge "being"; time, then, is of critical importance to all of Heidegger's career — from *The History of Time*, derived from a lecture course taught in 1925, through the turn of the 1930s, to the later writings on language.

It is common knowledge that Heidegger was, at best, pressured to publish *Being and Time* in order to keep his academic position; in a sense then, we can see the finished text as provisional, if not rushed. The final draft was written in just under a month, and indeed, Heidegger himself claimed that for much of his career what we now read as a completed text was only the "first" part. *Being and Time,* then, serves as a ground for a system purposely left unconstructed; it is the beginning of the clearing that Heidegger draws us back towards in his later writings, the space where the forest has been pushed back enough to allow for the lightening (*Lichtung*) to come forward. We can then begin to see his later work, his work after the turn (which is not so much a turn, as is often thought, in Heidegger's thinking so much *as a turn in thinking itself*) as always a return to the issues of *Sein* and *Zeit,* and of the questioning, repeated always, of the bare facticity that there is something rather than nothing. We will attempt here to continue to follow a *Holzweg* between Heidegger's conception(s) of time and Dōgen's, not so much to define how one influences the other (they don't influence so much as interpenetrate), but in a way that by understanding Heidegger's fluctuating concepts of temporality, *Augenblick, Ereignis,* and Dōgen's *uji,* we will be better able to understand the other through the first.

Heidegger's concern with time involves the very idea of being itself. As early as 1924 in a small text that could serve as first draft of *Being and Time* titled *History of the Concept of Time,* Heidegger states that "*Dasein itself* [...] is 'time.'"[9] Time and

---

9   Martin Heidegger, *History of the Concept of Time Prolegomena,* trans. Theodore Kiesel. (Indianapolis: Indiana University Press, 1985), 197.

thereby history (that through which we pass) is not merely a door through which we pass nor an ontological entity which passes us by, but is rather the very definition of being; it is not a separate thing from us. To be is not only to be within time, but indeed to be with time, or even to be time. In *Being and Time*'s introduction, Heidegger writes that "we shall point to temporality as the meaning of the Being of that entity which we shall call 'Dasein.'"[10] To understand Dasein, or "being-there," we must understand being's very real temporality; being is, in effect, being-temporary; to be is to be contingent, temporary, finite. To authentically understand our temporality is to go beyond the surface knowledge of one's mortality, and to understand being-there's profoundly contingent, temporally bounded, nature.

In order to understand these attempts to characterize time, it may be necessary to provide a background understanding of how time works. For most of our lives, we exist in a time that is broadly understood — it is perhaps a little boring in its predictability, as one moment follows the next. The Greeks referred to this time as *chronos* (from which we get chronological from); moment follows from moment, and what once was not yet is all too quickly already past. This is the time we know all too well, but the Greeks also imagined another time, which they referred to as the *kairos*. Kairotic time is the moment of the instant, and holds within itself an opening to the potential beingness of all things; it is timeliness (a moment of that moment, an instant of that instant). A.N. Whitehead called this time the time of the "creative advance." Kairotic time is the instant fulfillment of potential, and as such cannot be plotted or predicted; it is, at the risk of falling too far into the vague, an opening into what otherwise remains closed with the seriatic universe of chronological time.

For Heidegger, time informs — and forms — one's being through its indeterminate possibilities in relation to the three conventional stages of past, future, and present. Past, future,

---

10 Martin Heidegger, *Being and Time,* trans. John Macquarrie and Edward Robinson (New York: Harper & Row, 1962), 38.

and present are, in an everyday sense, separate "times" or individual phenomena; according to our prosaic senses, what is in the future must remain there until becoming something present and with that it is suddenly gone, reclassified as the past, where it must reside eternally. A common (mis)conception of time is that it is something we pass through or over — viewed this way, time is not us but a separate entity entirely. Aristotle struggles with this aporetic difficulty, asking "does [the now] always remain one and the same or is it always other and other?"[11] and in answer replying "if the 'now' were not different but one and the same, there would not have been time."[12]

Heidegger was writing against, and actively struggling with, Aristotle's conceptions of time. For Aristotle, time comports difference, change, alterity, fluctuation, and instability. Aristotle saw time as seriatim passage, predictable as "number of movement, according to before and after."[13] For Heidegger, authentic temporality remains a possibility and as such is very much a dynamic force. Temporality reaches into the future and extends to the past in a mode of ecstatic fluidity. It is not simply an interminable parade of now-points. Drawing on the new, more originary descriptions of time, Heidegger refers to these modes as "the ecstases of temporality."[14] In a footnote to *Being and Time,* Macquarrie and Robinson describe the root meaning of the word *ekstasis* as the mode of "standing outside," which lends a more precise cast to this idea; rather than being something rapturous (how we would normally define the word ecstasy), "standing outside" contains an inflection that removes us from the immediate nature of transformation; standing outside means we exist at a remove from something. By being removed (through standing in a clearing), we are able to observe it occurring; *we look in.* Heidegger describes the different forms of ecstatic time as inter-informed — "the future, the character of having been, and the

---

11 Aristotle, *Physics,* Book IV, 218.

12 Ibid.

13 Ibid

14 Heidegger, *Being and Time,* 377.

Present show the phenomenal characteristics of the 'towards-oneself', the 'back-to', and the 'letting-oneself-be-encountered-by'."[15] Rather than time existing as a separate entity which we encounter at one time, temporality is being-there's original Being. Being becomes manifest (to beings) through what could be called an interpenetration of times within times; time is in motion, and moves not only in a single direction. Time "allows" for the "factical potentiality-for-Being,"[16] or what becomes Dasein. We become aware of Being through the profound understanding of, or encounter with, our being's highly contingent nature. Indeed, Dasein only comes to be as a possibility through engagement with the fact of our futural finitude. That I will die, that this is not permanent, and, far more radically, that none of this perdures, and that everything that is, is contingent, exists as a source of dread to me; confronting the world at its very limit is horrifying, it is the ground of nihilism. However, that same horror also, in extreme cases, reveals another, primordial ground, a ground which liberates me for the first time from the prosaic, quotidian reality of crude, everyday life into an authentic encounter with Being, which is, in effect, not bound by the temporal, and which exists outside of — or above, or beyond — inauthentic conceptions of a correct and acceptable world view. This soteriological vault through horror is best illustrated through Kierkegaard's "mighty trampoline leap" in which true authentic belief only emerges through a confrontation and rejection of learned dogma, through a resistance to received knowledge in favor of a passional, perhaps illogical, response to that which cannot be known; for Kierkegaard, this is God.[17]

While a common everyday view of time views a future which passes through a "now" into the past in a unidirectional, constant flow, Heidegger's determination of time is significantly more nuanced; in Heidegger's "primordial temporality," the

---

15   Heidegger, *Being and Time,* 377.

16   Ibid., 372.

17   Søren Kierkegaard, *Fear And Trembling: Repetition,* trans. Howard V. Hong and Edna H. Hong (Princeton: Princeton University Press, 1983), 36.

question of the future is always informed by a past, and the past, or having-been, is of a concern for being-there. In *The Concept of Time,* Heidegger casts Dasein as a future possibility; Dasein is a "being out toward what is not yet, but can be."[18] Dasein views itself through its own possibilities — even the possibility of possibilities — and through its futural thrownness; being-there projects itself into what it desires and imagines itself *as a self* there. It reaches towards. This is not wishful thinking but a genuine (authentic) grappling with its own existential possibilities. This futural possibility is, however, inevitably informed by a past (past decisions, heritages, histories, etc.) and therefore this possibility of a future "draws" as well on a past, re-invigorating that past, reimagining it, but making it something unequivocally, defiantly, no longer past. Heidegger writes in *Being and Time* that "only in so far as Dasein is as an 'I-am-as-having-been', can Dasein come towards itself futurally in such a way that it comes back."[19] Being and beings are reunited — become unalienated and return as one — through authentic engagement with the question of beings's contingent finitude. Being-there becomes through what it was, as much as what it will become. It reaches both into the past and the future, becoming now through its past facticity and futural possibilities. Heidegger continues "As authentically futural, Dasein is authentically as 'having been' [...] the character of 'having been' arises, in a certain way, from the future."[20] Being-there is, Heidegger writes, because of what it was; the future be-comes because of the past. Time, then, is not a unidirectional street from the future into the past; rather it effects and informs itself *as it comes to be.*

How then do we come to view time, not in the conditioned everydayness of common, "vulgar," chronological reality, but within the ecstatic dimensions of *kairotic* temporality which exist, so far, as possibility, and more importantly, why does it

---

18 Martin Heidegger, *The Concept of Time,* trans. Ingo Farin (London: Continuum Publishing, 2011), 48.

19 Heidegger, *Being and Time,* 373.

20 Ibid.

matter? For Heidegger, especially in *Being and Time,* but, as we shall see as well in *Contributions,* we attain a new understanding (we begin again) of being-there's fundamental approach through "anticipatory resoluteness," through a "standing-in." By projecting ourselves towards a future (which is informed by the past) which we are not sure about, we experience the "ecstasy" of anticipation; we find ourselves resolved in our expectation, thus leaving open, or allowing to come (forth), that futural experience which, if we were to remain closed down, cannot come forward. For Heidegger, anticipatory resoluteness is "authentic Being towards the possibility which we have characterized as Dasein's utter impossibility."[21] The idea that Dasein's existence is not temporal is "an impossibility," but one which we seek safety in everyday; to remain "authentic" we must recognize not an end as such, but that Dasein as being "exists finitely." This is the radical stance of anticipatory resoluteness; to recognize in Dasein's "utter impossibility" not a nihilistic surrender but the chance to prepare oneself for a new beginning. Few, as we have noted elsewhere, are prepared for such a challenge; "*only the rare,*" Heidegger writes in the *Contributions,* "who are endowed with great courage" can place themselves on the path of thinking finitude with any authentic resolve.[22] This is not mere resolve born from a stoic nihilism, but rather a revolutionary attunement of being that is profound and born from a certain attuned and enlightened horror at being's sudden finitude.

The Time in Contributions

In *Contributions,* Heidegger's treatment of time changes (but again, we can begin perhaps to see this as a rethinking of his earlier considerations, a provisional restatement of an incipient thinking-towards begun early in the century and carried for-

---

21 Ibid., 378.

22 Martin Heidegger, *Contribution to Philosophy (Of the Event),* trans. Richard Rojcewicz and Daniela Vallega-Neu (Bloomington: Indiana University Press, 2012), 12.

ward through the thrusts and feints of what Blanchot will call the disaster of the 20th century), and this is yet again a sign of how Heidegger's own thinking replicates his call towards a new beginning. In *Contributions,* Heidegger describes his stance (to the question of the "meaning of Being")[23] as essentially un-changed from that of *Being and Time*; only "the positions of the questioning are constantly different."[24] Yet as we begin (*again*) to question "more originally," the nature of questioning changes radically, though not necessarily the essence of the questioning. Before claiming mastery of an entire system, we need to begin with the preliminaries, and it is so often the preliminaries — the originary beginnings — where thinking at its most essential is birthed, and where it is first interrogated. This is where Hei-degger resists easy interpretations and simplistic conceptual-izations; Heidegger himself practices, as an ethics of thought, a constant return to the incipient beginnings he calls us towards in his writing. It is in the preliminaries where the main points are broached and understood, and Heidegger returns to again and again as the originary question — the question that is of a concern for us — that we have not yet *begun to think* — the ques-tion of thinking.

Yet what we have described here so far, has, to a large degree, been, in Heidegger's words, "blind, useless, and bereft of any ac-tual, philosophizing question."[25] We have merely picked out and strung "together 'passages' in which some problem or other is discussed."[26] We have not yet begun to think the question. In order to understand the disclosures of the event of truth, we must examine in depth, with Heidegger, the advent of the event, and more importantly, (the) space and (the) time in which it can occur. While an entire study or career could be made of examining the pathways of thinking that Heidegger exposes in the *Contributions,* for our purposes, within this chapter, we will

---

23 Following the style of Rojcewicz and Vallega-Neu, we will take for *Seyn* their translation henceforth as "Being."

24 Heidegger, *Contribution to Philosophy (Of the Event),* 67.

25 Ibid., 299.

26 Ibid.

restrict ourselves to a single section — that of chapter v, entitled "The Grounding" which looks to the emergence of "Da-sein," "truth," and "time-space" in the new beginning — in an attempt to understand his *Holzweg,* which is as much ours, towards another grounding, which ends, if it does, only within the domain of the abyssal. That this grounding is one that never grounds, that never becomes *essence* is of a concern for us.

Da-sein

Yet how abyssally cleared must the clearing for self-concealing be, such that withdrawal might not appear superficially as mere nullity but might reign as bestowal.[27]

The concept of Dasein changes in *Contributions* and marks the most profound shift — or at least evolution — in Heidegger's thinking Being and beings in the decade since *Being and Time* was first published. Dasein here becomes Da-sein, and, as the hyphenation indicates, is no longer concerned with the possibility of beings encounter with Being, as such, but attends instead to the profound possibility of the event of truth, or of disclosure of truth to being, through its encounter with Being; the emphasis of the word changes from *being*-there, to being-*there* (from Da-*Sein* to Da-sein). Heidegger's concern is with the there of Being's disclosure, the site of its presencing, which acts as the event of truth, or *Ereignis.* No longer is Dasein simply a possibility; it becomes, through Da-sein, being's exposure to Being within the "*there*" of truth's evental truthing. There is a great deal of language at play here, and it is critical to note that for the Heidegger of the *Contributions* (even more so than in *Being and Time*), the need of a system of the logical and the rational has been laid to rest; Heidegger is speaking towards the question from within a sense of awe, rather than answering it with a certainty. As such, we will need to restrict our understanding to a thinking with, or thinking towards, rather than a knowing as such. Thinking with the *Contributions* leaves behind the

---

27 Ibid., 231.

Socratic certainty of the syllogism and returns thinking to the place of the wonder of Parmenides and Heraclitus. From that rejection to the claim of edifical knowledge comes an embrace towards the uncertainty of Being's *be-*coming within the site of the rejection, within the openness of the event of truth.

The disclosure of *Ereignis* happens no longer in a grounding which is rooted in a world of "Christian saeculum" but rather occurs in a more original, abyssally located fissure through which the event of truth comes forward not by force and naming, but of its ownmost authenticity.[28] This fissure is a break in the known; rather than certainty what emerges is the uncertain. It is important to note that the uncertain is in no way the unclear; the uncertain has the quality of a deep abiding, a dwelling-in which gives forth, through practice, a brilliant quality of knowing. Heidegger writes that "in *Being and Time,* Dasein still has an appearance that is 'anthropological', 'subjectivistic', 'individualistic',"[29] but that in this new reading of the term, as we read it in the *Contributions,* Da-sein is as a das Sein des Da, or the being of the there, with this there-being "the openness of beings as such and as a whole, the ground of the more originarily conceived Ἀλήθεια [*Alētheia*]."[30] Da-sein, as the there of being-there is the grounding of truth in "this simplest of fissure[s]."[31] As we read "The Grounding" carefully we will begin to see what Heidegger means by fissures, and of the different conditions, or manifestations, of ground as not only ground, but abyssal ground and primordial ground. The presence of the abyss, into which we both leap freely, as well as find ourselves thrown toward, is by its very nature a groundless ground, and this has the effect of radically leaving open "the question of Being" to be asked again "in the new beginning."

Read this way, being-there opens itself to the event of truth through an act of clearing away the inherited misconceptions

---

28 Ibid., 233.
29 Ibid.
30 Ibid., 234.
31 Ibid.

from the history of metaphysics, of the misconceptions birthed in "that other beginning." (Now we are beginning to think, if only hesitatingly.) Like a form of "anticipatory resoluteness," the human being who is grounded in "steadfastness," who grounds oneself *as a practice,* and within the practice of thinking the other beginning, allows for the presencing of the event of truth to open, or disclose itself, to them. This steadfastness (which reads as a preparatory or initial *Gelassenheit,* or releasement, a term Heidegger does not think in any formal way until roughly eight years after the initial writing of *Contributions*[32]) is like a clearing and, like a literal forest clearing, must be attended to, cleared and prepared. Heidegger writes:

> The steadfast enduring of the clearing of self-concealing is taken up in the seeking, preserving, and stewardship carried out by that human being who has the self-knowledge as one appropriated to being and belonging to the event qua the essential occurrence of Being.[33]

To practice the steadfast enduring, the staying with, that the clearing calls us towards requires a careful practice and "stewardship" by the person who is already self-aware. This is not a revelatory moment of sudden "seeing" in the history of religious attunement; rather the exposure of being to Being requires a persistent training towards this event, a waiting "on that which answers pure waiting" in the dialogic language of the "Evening Conversation." Through practice, beings, when met with an open clearing, are prepared to experience the event of truth truthing and do not stumble past this clearing blindly.

In preparation for this event of the grounding of Da-sein, Heidegger advises in *Contributions* the cultivating of four practices, or virtues; the first, "strength" works not as a simple, mere

---

32 Despite the appearance of *Gelassenheit* in numerous forms prior to *Country Path Conversations,* the term itself in "inherited" from Meister Eckhardt and as such was already part of the German philosophical lexicon. We will examine Heidegger's thinking of *Gelassenheit* in a subsequent chapter.

33 Heidegger, *Contributions to Philosophy (Of the Event),* 235.

accrual of power; rather strength is seen as "the mastery of the free bestowal of the broadest fields of creative self-surpassing."[34] This can be read as allowing oneself — through a strength as mastery — to creatively remain open to the moment of "self-surpassing." That is, as a practice to *practice* the recognition that one always exceeds the known. The second virtue, "decisiveness," is practiced not through obstinacy, or stubbornness, but rather through "the security of belonging to the event, the entry into the unprotected."[35] Opening oneself to the possibility of being unprotected — from within the unknown — is a hallmark of the leap; we can read here again the surrender of letting go; to let oneself go is to fall unprotected from the confines of safety; it is *to decide to fall.* The third virtue, "mildness," is not to be confused with "the weakness of leniency" (we can read Nietzsche here). Mildness instead, for Heidegger, is the "generous wakening of the concealed and retained, that which ever strangely binds all creating into what is essential to creating."[36] Instead of directing us towards a Christian timidity, the form of mildness that Heidegger invokes here advises one to practice a restraint in naming the world, in building an inauthentic edifice over the uncertainty of the fissure. By practicing restraint, we allow that which is "creative" to *be*-come the creative. This is done not through an act of positive assertion, or claiming, but through its ownmost originary, essential force of being *be*-coming. Finally, Heidegger names "simplicity" as the fourth virtue, one which is not meant to be confused with the "futureless" nor the easy, but in "the passion for the necessity of the single task of securing the inexhaustibility of Being in the shelter of beings and not letting go of the strangeness of Being."[37] Simplicity directs us towards the new beginning which returns us, in turn, to the awe and wonder of thinking that Heidegger has traced to existing before Plato, before Socrates, before the onslaught of metaphysical and

---

34 Ibid.
35 Ibid.
36 Ibid., 236.
37 Ibid.

scientific answering. We must never let the strangeness — of existence, of life, of world — go; to do so risks enmeshing being in an unreal, alienated, and withdrawn existence, to an inauthentic existence already formed, already answered, already taken up and in which we find ourselves already thrown upon. Taken together, these four practices work to direct and "ground" being as being-there, there in the "steadfast enduring of the clearing, i.e., of the freed, unprotected and belonging domain of the 'there' wherein Being conceals itself."[38] Be-ing is disclosed as being-there within the event of truth through a practice of the four traits of strength, decisiveness, mildness, and simplicity which amount to a practice of "steadfast enduring."

Heidegger is careful in the *Contributions* to "allow" for Dasein to evolve from a mere "anthropological" concept grasped only in relation to the human being as he views the Dasein of *Being and Time,* into what eems to functionwithin the "between." Before we describe what he means by the "between," we must continue to understand the very specific meaning of Dasein that Heidegger is trying to describe. It is important, again, to understand what Heidegger is describing is in motion, in flux. It is not an isolated concept which can be readily defined and named; we can only claim to understand it provisionally. Heidegger writes that though Da-sein could never be named in an "immediate 'description,'" as if it "were simply to be found objectively present somewhere," it can and should be found

> in a rightly understood projection which brings forth the contemporary human being, even if only in abandonment by being and prepares the resonating of the fact that the human being is the being which has broken out into the open.[39]

Da-sein is not — in contrast to a traditionally conceived God — a separate entity that gives being Being, nor is it being itself; rather, Da-sein, in flux, in movement, creates the opening (*das Of-*

---

38 Ibid., 235.
39 Ibid., 246.

fen) for being to *be*-come, even if this being is within the midst of the plight of the abandonment by Being. The event "opens up" in the space between — according to an illustration in *Contributions*[40] — Human Being and Gods, World and Earth. Da-sein exists as being-there in a central pivot through which the event of truth as appropriation sunders common reality, the reality based in that first beginning, and which must make a break with contemporary existence in order to allow for the more authentic, more primordial other beginning which, to Heidegger, is as much a site of "strife" as it is an edenic truth. Da-sein withstands "as an essential occurrence of the truth of Being,"[41] as a space between two beginnings, between humans and gods; in this way it is not its ownmost site for truth, nor is it separate from truth. It occurs as the space between, and this between must be looked at more closely.

Truth

It is only in these fissured, abyssal spaces — spaces which are indeed non-spaces — spaces which are groundless (which *resist* the grounding), that Heidegger proposes that any element of the unveiling, or remembering, of truth can appear. This happens in the open (*das Offen*) of the cleared space where the evental disclosure of the event of truth, the event of appropriation — the making, or rather claiming, of something its own-most — can occur. It is exceedingly difficult to describe these "events" chronologically; as we have already seen, the "event" of inceptual thinking takes place in the leap, yet the leap could not, would not, occur authentically had not the event of thinking already begun. This is what Heidegger means by inceptual; in this new world of the new beginning, everything is inceptual, provisional; it is both the hesitancy of the *Contributions* and the anticipatoriness of *Being and Time*. It is the self-withholding of being-there in expectation of the incipient belonging to Being that occurs in

---

40 Ibid.
41 Ibid.

the sudden moment of authentic presence (*Augenblick*), a moment that beings have been preparing for, through the practice listed above.

While an entire study could be taken up with the idea of *alētheia*, or the disclosure(s) of truth as the site of being, for our purposes we will again restrict Heidegger's conceptions of the term to a single section of the *Contributions*. Here, Heidegger traces the genealogical etymology of the word "truth" from its "first beginnings" immersed in pre-Socratic "awe" and "wonder" to its eventual impoverishment as a term more closely "yoked" to a correctness and rule-following from which Heidegger proposes to rescue or re-ground it. The concept of truth as an uncovering, or as an appropriation of its self to its ownmost, only emerges within the opening or clearing; it is towards that end that we will pursue the understanding.

For Heidegger, the question of truth always remains a question as important as the question of Being. It is only through, as we shall see, the event of truth disclosing itself that being-there is understood as a unity with Being, and it is not seen as separate, disparate, possibly inauthentic and possibly all-pervading entity. While Heidegger uses various words throughout his career to describe the event, we cannot understand the concept without first an understanding of the word — *alētheia* — which he uses most often to describe it. For Heidegger, *alētheia*, which he takes to mean both truth and the event, is the event of truth as it comes to be. The word describes that which comes forward, or is disclosed, with and within the evental site. *Alētheia* returns to truth its original self through the event of appropriation, or making something one's ownmost. Is *alētheia* then the event itself? *Alētheia* as the disclosure of truth cannot come forward without first a clearing of the evental site, but, just as importantly, the site itself always presages the already undisclosed nature of *alētheia*; both come to be co-originarily, and neither precedes the other. Both already exist, and it is through an attunement — to the moment, to Being — as well as a "letting-be," that they come to be experienced. This sudden attunement to the event as it comes to be is Heidegger's understanding of *kai-*

rotic time, that time mentioned above in which an opening occurs which propels da-sein out of mundane chronological time.

Heidegger traces the meaning of *alētheia* back to its etymological origins (which, for Heidegger is always more than an etymological journey, and inevitably serves as a way to understand the ground of a word, to better understand our comportment toward the meaning of the word). As already discussed, *alētheia,* operating as an a-privative in Greek, refers to truth as a "disclosure" or an "unconcealedness" and refers always to the "whence and wherefore [of] concealment and unconcealment."[42] The term aletheia draws its inspiration form the river Lethe of Greek mythology, one of the five rivers of Hades underground world; all who drank from it forgot completely their previous lives aboveground. Lethe then is the river of forgetting; the word itself means either "oblivion" or "concealment." *Alētheia,* as the privative *alpha,* thus becomes the "remembering" of truth (or the forgetting of what was forgotten, and the remembering of what was to be remembered.) Truth then becomes a rescuing from oblivion of what was loss, and an unconcealment of what had been concealed. In this sense, *alētheia* is opposed to a more Western notion of truth as something unchanging and based in fact, and takes on instead the notion of action.

Heidegger discusses *alētheia* in his first substantial discussion of the term in his essay from "The Origin of the Work of Art," written roughly two years before *Contributions.*[43] In the "Origin," Heidegger equates *alētheia* with "the unconcealment of beings" and an "essence of truth[44] that flashes out [with]in the word."[45] While truth as unconcealment existed as a possibility in early Greek thinking, it has, Heidegger writes, been eclipsed

---

42 Ibid., 261.

43 Heidegger writes "The Origin of the Work of Art" over a span of two years, from roughly 1935 through 1937, and reworked it for publication in 1950, and again in 1960.

44 We will see that this "flash" of Heidegger's will be of critical concern below as we discuss Augenblick and satori.

45 Martin Heidegger, *Basic Writings,* ed. David Farrell Krell (New York: Harper & Row, 1977), 176.

by equating truth with "correctness," which, in effect, creates a false edifice of "truth as certainty." By exploring the concept of truth as unconcealment or disclosure, "we are reminding ourselves of what, unexperienced and unthought, underlies our familiar and therefore outworn essence of truth in the sense of correctness."[46] When we expose ourselves to the possibility of truth as a "remembering," we remove it from something we "make" or "create"; truth as disclosure becomes, in effect, a more primordial — *abyssal* — ground on which to base the essential openness of wonder and awe. Truth as a ground has always existed, yet only always as withdrawn, abyssal ground; in this, one cannot make truth, but only clear a space through which it may emerge. The act of metaphysical releasement takes place without God, without a correct bearing; it is an opening of beings to the possibility of Being, to the possibility of possibility itself. In "Origin," Heidegger writes:

> Things are, and human beings, gifts and sacrifices are, animals and plants are, equipment and works are. The particular being stands in Being. Through Being there passes a veiled fatality that is ordained between the godly and the countergodly. There is much in being that man cannot master. There is but little that comes to be known. What is known remains inexact, what is mastered insecure. Beings are never of our own making, or even merely our representations, as it might all too easily seem. When we contemplate this whole as one, then we apprehend, so it appears, all that is — though we grasp it crudely enough.[47]

Truth is never absent, but is always withdrawn, undisclosed; *alētheia* brings forward the disclosure as an encounter, an encounter which occurs "in its essential extent as the openness of being."[48] *Alētheia* is the remembering of the authentic being-

---

46 Ibid., 177.
47 Ibid., 178.
48 Heidegger, *Contributions to Philosophy (Of the Event),* 261.

there which is always already a possibility. In *Contributions,* Heidegger writes that *a-lētheia* means "un-concealment and the un-concealed itself." While *alētheia* may mean this originally, the claims of metaphysical certainties have corrupted this term, denying truth "openness" and replacing it with "correctness." Heidegger writes that, at the end of this history of truth as correctness,

> All that remains as first and last is conformity, rectitudo, and within this determination an explanation of "correctness must be sought out of the respective interpretation of the human being (as soul) and of beings, provided "correctness" is not altogether taken as purely and simply self-evident.[49]

By artificially "yoking" the concept of truth to "correctness," truth is robbed of its originary authenticity; what is correct has replaced what is authentically true. Things — as undisclosed, partial entities — are not true at all but are instead enmeshed endlessly in inauthentic relations with the "perceiver to things."[50] The truth of something becomes a handmaiden to one's perception of the thing, and no longer has as its own its own appropriation. This, in effect, reduces the entire notion of truth to the "correctness" of a perception. It is not, however, to the originary, primordial event of truth's disclosure. The term *alētheia* returns to truth its original, primordial meaning.

In the *Contributions,* Heidegger answers, provisionally, in §213, "What the question of truth is about."[51] To arrive at the more originary, more primordial event of truth that the encounter with *alētheia* brings forth is to understand that what truth means is "not about a mere modification of the concept," nor even a "more original insight into the essence" of the thing or event.[52] Rather, for Heidegger, one's exposure to the question of

---

49 Ibid., 265.
50 Ibid., 264.
51 Ibid., 267.
52 Ibid.

truth opens one into possibility, into what he calls "the leap into the essential occurrence of truth."[53] This leap into an authentic encounter at once results in "a transformation of the human being in a sense of a dis-lodging of its position and beings."[54] The transformation is a grounding, which, as a fundamental action, "empowers" being-there "itself as event."[55] Being-there is the evental *be*-coming of the event itself which is "above all the grounding of the human being in Da-sein as the ground required by Being itself for its own truth."[56] What we are seeing here is an essential occurring of being's joining to Being as being-there (Da-sein), not in the sense of a reunification or of a divisible two becoming one, but through a recognition that — within the primordial, and originarily — Da-sein is the possibility of an essential wholeness that discloses itself repeatedly as the event of truth.

Within the schema of what Heidegger refers to as "the usual horizon of 'logic' and of the predominant thinking,"[57] the projection of the grounding of truth remains arbitrary. Science, as logic, creates an artificial ground upon which the essence or basis of "truth" is projected; this only serves to maintain an artificial barrier to the presencing of an authentic truth. It remains false and unstable and "truth is taken as an object of calculation and computation, and ultimate intelligibility by an everyday machinational understanding is claimed as the measure."[58] However, for Heidegger, this interpretation of "truth" as a measure of world fails disastrously by creating an "arbitrary ground" upon which we build "stable" answers to questions, and where we falsely answer the original question. Heidegger writes:

> Truth for us is also not what is firmly established, that suspicious offspring of validities in themselves. Nor is it the mere

---

53 Ibid.
54 Ibid., 268.
55 Ibid.
56 Ibid.
57 Ibid., 260.
58 Ibid.

opposite, the crude and constant flux of all opinions. Truth is the abyssal center which trembles in the passing of the god and thus is the withstood ground for the grounding of creative Da-sein.[59]

Truth exists as an in between, as a trembling center into which can flow, and does flow, the essential occurrence (which is different than the essence) of the event. The trembling center, by being precisely nowhere but "in between," allows for something to come to be, to be-come. This occurs by way of a ground which only provisionally acts as a ground, as a "withstood ground." Heidegger proposes locating the clearing as merely a provisional, fugacious site. He directs us towards a ground which has been temporarily delineated and laid out in order to prepare the site for the eventual event of truth to take place; that it is provisional is not a detriment, but indeed necessary to begin to anticipate an authentic relation to truth.

In a long paragraph which deserves to be cited in its entirety, Heidegger draws us towards something with which Dōgen is comfortable (but which the history of Western metaphysics remains decidedly uncomfortable). This is the concept of emptiness, of the space for nothing, or more accurately, *no thing*. It is critical here to point out that our reading of *no thing* follows a Buddhistic notion equating nothingness not to the meaninglessness of nihilism, but rather as a soteriological "opening" into a new beginning, an other place; it is the clearing which we have been practicing clearing, which all practice inexorably leads towards, and through, an opening towards the event of truth surges forth. For Heidegger, it is where no thing exists, perdures, manifests, that is precisely the space (of no-thing-ness) where the truth of things — as the event of appropriation — can come to be known; it is the clearing, and it is the openness, and it is the space of no thing, through which things — in their authentic, deeply original selves — can presence themselves. Heidegger writes that this is not a truly empty realm;

---

59 Ibid., 262.

the open realm, which conceals itself at the same time that beings have come to stand in it in each case [.... It] is in fact something like the inner recess, e.g., that of a jug. Yet it must be recognized that the inner recess is not just an haphazard emptiness which arises purely on account of the surrounding walls and which happens not to be full of "things." It is just the opposite: the inner recess itself is what determines, shapes, and bears the walling action of the walls and of their surfaces. The walls and surfaces are merely what is radiated out by that original open realm which allows its openness to come into play by summoning up, round about itself and toward itself, such-and-such walls (the particular form of the vessel). That is how the essential occurrence of the open realm radiates back from and in the embracing walls.[60]

This is not to say, for Heidegger, that there was no thing there, within the jug. Heidegger is drawing us towards the idea that within this space of no thing, there is not-a-thing per se, but that the *no-thing* — which is the event of truth — occurs as an in between, *between* the walling actions of the jug (or presenting phenomena). Heidegger writes that, despite it being no thing and no being exactly "it pertains to being itself and is the trembling of the event of the self-concealing."[61] This is where, in the space of no space, that truth itself comes to rest, comes to be, where the event of truth, as a truthing event, discloses itself only (with)-in no thing-ness.

And yet, within this disclosure is the concealedness of being-there which remains within the opening of the disclosure. The concealed is only partially ever overcome, so that within this space of no thing, what is there must remain always partially withdrawn. We come to *know* the event only provisionally, as an incipient beginning, beginning again; our very encounter is partial, fragmentary but this very act is what it means to begin to think. The leap is inevitably a leap into an unknown, and indeed

---

60 Ibid., 268.

61 Ibid.

must be; it is a surrender into a tradition that is not a tradition at all, that destroys traditions as ideas, and which rests its own grounding on the authentic event of truth which happens in the abyssal between.

Time-Space (*Zeit-raum*)

But where then is the "there" of being-there? In what space, primordial or otherwise does there manifest itself? Can something come from where there is nothing? Even in the quivering between — a fissured remnant — is there not space? (Here we can recall Nietzsche, who, perhaps describing Zarathustra in his short "The Parable of a Madman," writes, in the famous passage on the death of God, "*Are we not straying into an infinite nothing? Do we not feel the breath of empty space? Has it not become colder?*"[62]) For Heidegger, the event of truth manifests and comes to be within the "space" of time-space (*Zeit-raum*). This space is not a Kantian category, an irremovable set of goggles that must exist *a priori* to our experiencing of the truth. Space and time are normally conceived and defined through the postulations of "physics," and leaves time, as a concept, a mere "fourth parameter," a fourth wall on which the edifices of modern scientific thinking are founded, and in which the radical concepts of space and time "have already been leveled down to the sameness of what is calculable and what makes calculation possible."[63] Even here Heidegger has changed the formula, reversing the standard equation of space and time (and hyphenating the words). For Heidegger, time-space is where space and time "each represented for itself and in their usual conjunction" arise from.[64] Time-space is "more originary than [space and time] themselves and than their calculatively represented conjunction."[65]

---

62 Friedrich Nietzsche, *The Gay Science,* trans. Walter Kaufman (New York: Random House, 1974), 181.

63 Ibid., 298.

64 Ibid., 294.

65 Ibid.

In this sense, space and time are controlled and ordered in such a way as to make sense of the world (rather than leaving open the question, the question which is *most* question-worthy). This approach ignores the more "originary," and therefore more fundamental, conception of the unity of time and space as a possible site in which the unity serves as a provisional and abyssal ground for the coming to be, or emergence, of the truth of Being in the form of an historical *be*-coming. This is only possible if, at least initially and provisionally, we uncouple the concepts of time and space from each other to first identify the essence "of each, clarified as properly as its own" and examine within each concept both its "extreme separateness" and that each arises from something shared and "originary."[66] This originary source is common to each as a root is common to the shoots of a plant (yet remains different.) This common root acts as a "root-grounding ground" and "the essence of truth."[67] The difficulty, if we refuse this, is that we will never arrive at the "ground" in which the event of truth is located. We will always refuse the call *towards* being-there, and always be already thinking what has previously been thought, cogitating about the known rather than leaping into a new, in Heidegger's words, "abyssal ground."

The "abyssal ground," for Heidegger, is the "*originary unity* of space and time," the unity which "allows" them to "diverge into their separateness."[68] This same abyssal ground is the "originary essence of the ground," and as such, is "*of the essence of truth.*" The abyssal ground is also "the staying away of the ground." If we were to illustrate this notion, we might imagine ground being an "ungrounded" temporary, provisional support hovering somewhere above a purely opened space which, as the abyssal ground, is in the process of always withdrawing, always separating itself from the provisional ground, always already "staying away."[69] The two grounds, though intimately giving each other

---

66 Ibid., 298.

67 Ibid.

68 Ibid.

69 Ibid., 299.

being, are always in a process of magnetic-like repulsion, resist-ing their unification and joining. Heidegger writes that "inas-much as the ground, even and precisely as abyss, still grounds and yet does not properly ground, it abides in hesitancy."[70] This is not a refusal entirely, however; the provisional "hesitancy" to-wards a saying of the definite, of stating an absolute, keeps them in this abyssal sway towards each other, even as it holds them apart. Heidegger writes:

> The abyssal ground is the hesitant self-withholding of the ground. In this withholding, the originary emptiness opens up and the originary *clearing* occurs, but this clearing is such that, at the same time, hesitation is manifest in it.[71]

Within this abyss where hesitancy looms, an emptiness is opened into, but this emptiness is decidedly not a negative space; rather it represents a fullness, or at least the possibility of a fullness. It is as though, within the abyss, everything that is, every thing that occurs within the quotidian, crude world of the everyday, drains away and is replaced by an originary "yawn-ing" emptiness, which, like the *no thing-ness* already mentioned, "allows" to come an entirely new beginning, a new thinking towards the event of an authentic experiencing of the truth as disclosure. This is not an emptiness "in the sense of sheer ab-sence of things," but rather an emptiness that *allows,* that gives to being Being through its "originary yawning open in hesitant self-withholding."[72] It is the "attuned disposing of the essential *dis-lodgments* of precisely *this* cleared being which allows such self-concealing to stand within it."[73] Opening being-*there* to the *there* located in the fissured opening of emptiness lets being-there be there as authentic beingness. Emptiness, Heidegger continues, "is actually the fullness of what is still undecided and

---

70 Ibid., 300.
71 Ibid.
72 Ibid., 301.
73 Ibid.

is to be decided, the abyssal ground that points to the ground, i.e., to the truth of being."[74] Emptiness is not a negative concept, but rather, like the jug, fulfills the plight of the abandoned being by "allowing" itself to give. Emptiness is the originary gift of the abyssal grounding of no thing. For a "thing" to come forward, it must have the space to (be)come; emptiness, effected through the withdrawal of phenomena from the clearing, is "offered" as a site for the be-coming, or disclosure of, *alētheia*.

Within the yawning fissure or gap, within this opening, originarily occurs time-space (*Zeit-raum*), which exists, as an abyssal ground for what will eventually become "space and time." Time and space, as a singularity, originally "'are not" writes Heidegger. Rather, "they essentially occur."[75] They occur as a "hesitant withholding" that grows out of an "intimation" (*der Wink*). This *Wink,* or hint towards, grows itself out of an "e-mergence" (*Ent-springen*) in the abyssal grounding of the essential occurrence of truth.[76] Time and space exist as categories, but only as the product of this original occurrence of time-space be-coming. What has occurred within this site is a captivating (of the "abyssal embrace of the gathering"[77]) and a transporting (of the "abyssal gathering into the embrace"[78]). Heidegger writes that, "time spatializes and is never captivating."[79] What is meant here is that time, as its originary form, works as a "countercurrent" and by being time, allows for space to exist as a grounding of the "embrace." He continues: "Space temporalizes and is never transporting."[80] As a countercurrent, again, the existence of space as an abyssal ground, allows time to come to be as a grounding of the "gathering." Heidegger continues:

---

74 Ibid., 302.
75 Ibid., 304.
76 Ibid., 305.
77 Ibid.
78 Ibid.
79 Ibid.
80 Ibid.

Time-space is the gathering embrace that captivates and transports at once; it is the abyssal ground which is structured in this way, which disposes accordingly, and whose essential occurrence becomes historical in the grounding of the "there" by Da-*sein* (by its essential paths of sheltering the truth).[81]

Time-space occurs as the original site of the be-coming of truth, and has almost nothing to do with our common, contemporary understanding of time and space, though, according to Heidegger, it does "contain a development, toward an understanding of these terms."[82] But does this not mean that *Zeit-raum* is simply a reformulation of a system of categories (Kantian or otherwise) in which an *a priori* ground is formulated, a ground which is not abyssal at all but in fact simply "resets" where, ontologically, Heidegger chooses to hang his hat?

Though an attempt to answer this question definitively would take more time (and space) than this study can anticipate, it is critical to note that Heidegger is not unaware of this problem. He writes, as though in response to our concern, that "the opening of the abyssal ground is not groundless." It is not simply a "no" to every conception of a ground. It is, rather, a yes "to the ground in the concealed breadth and remoteness of that ground." An affirmation, then, towards nothing, but not to the corrosive nothing of nihilism; instead then it is an extreme yes to the opening of nothing into absolute emptiness. We are in a place of regression, but not a negative regression. It is an "oscillating site of the moment,"[83] through a constant shifting (of sands, of grounds), through a refusal to state, or accept, the absolute as an Absolute. The abyssal is always already provisional, dynamic, in flux; it operates in a temporary "between" of fissured grounds, in the infinite nothing of Nietzsche's primordial question (do we not feel the breath of empty space?) Heidegger

---

81 Ibid.
82 Ibid.
83 Ibid., 306.

writes that "the abyssal ground is thus the inherently temporalizing, spatializing, and oscillating site of the moment for the 'between' and Da-sein must be grounded in this 'between.'"[84] The abyssal ground is not a negative, endless falling away; it is, instead, a place which refuses the already said, the already formulated, which questions, and most importantly, which thinks *that which is most question-worthy.*

Between

We have mentioned the "between" several times already and we should pause, if only temporarily, to explore this idea in Heidegger (and with the thought of comparing Heidegger's thinking with that of Dōgen, later). Da-sein, we have already said is not an entity, nor is it a site, though arguably it works, at times, as such. Instead, the encounter with being-there comes to be, in the in-between, *between* the projected entities of human beings and gods, world and earth. The between is the site (though it is not — it is a juncture, a joining or even a jointed encounter —) of strife and appropriation and is presaged by the leap. The leap into what? Precisely, it is the leap into the *between* that is itself seen as a "semblance of utter recklessness"[85] but which actually holds itself in a "steadfastness in withstanding the most remote nearness of the hesitant withholding."[86] Rather than a leap towards something, as in Kierkegaard's "leap to faith," Heidegger's leap is a "first penetration into the domain of the *history of being.* In the same sense that Da-sein is neither being, nor is it separate from being. Da-sein equally is not a geographical place, but operates as a sort of "place holder" for the withstanding or standing-in of being, for being's *sudden* intrusion. This is akin to the reticence that thinking must practice in order to allow, or to facilitate, the "place" of truth to occur. This returns us to the practices of strength, decisiveness, mildness, and simplicity; our

---

84 Ibid.
85 Ibid., 179.
86 Ibid.

leap into the between is controlled and withheld, embraced only to be released, to be let go.

The "between" space of Da-sein's coming to be (and the place of our leap) is within the fissure (*between the leap, into the abyss*). The fissure occurs as a result of the leap; these two cannot be separated. Heidegger writes that the fissure "is the inner, incalculable splitting open of the *ap-propriation,* i.e., the splitting open of the essential occurrence of Being."[87] This occurs with the possibility of the leap (and the leap is only possible within the possibility of an opening, the fissure, the "plight" of abandonment) and works as an "appropriating event" which "consigns god to the human being, even while it assigns the human being to god."[88] Da-sein, and thereby the human being, "are grounded abyssally in the event" through the leap, through the fissure.[89]

If we are going to be charged with thinking (in) a new beginning, the site of this confrontation with the *between* is not to be underestimated, indeed, it is critical. The *in between,* the site-less site of the impassioned withholding of power to allow for that which has withdrawn to *re-*appear is exactly not indeterminate as a something between; indeed, in its very *noth*ingness (as opposed to its *some*thingness), the *between* operates as a juncture (*Fugen*)[90] between beginnings. This *between* grounds, for Heidegger, the occurrence of the event of Being, and (it is important not to deny the poetry that is at work in Heidegger's writing) the "self-opening center" which, within the *in between,* "makes the gods and humans decidable for one another."[91] The *in between,* as such, is indescribable in terms of entity or system-

---

87 Ibid., 220.

88 Ibid.

89 Ibid.

90 According to Parvis Emad and Kenneth Maly's translation, "juncture" (*Fugen*) is translated as "jointing." (Martin Heidegger, *Contributions to Philosophy (From Enowning),* trans. Parvis Emad and Kenneth Maly [Bloomington: Indiana University Press, 1999], xvii). That may, in this rare case, work better than the more contemporary translation.

91 Heidegger, *Contributions to Philosophy (Of the Event),* 247.

atized processing. The in between occurs as an event through the fissuring of the concrete, concretized ways of being; far from being indeterminate, it is a landslide, an earthquake; behind me a stable predictable, inauthentic world — ahead, the passional plight of the new beginning *in between* the not yet known, the unnamed. It is into this abyss that the leap (*that most daring venture in the course of inceptual thinking*)[92] takes us; instead of being thrown into a world, projected as an inauthentic being into a world perpetually undisclosed and without truth, we (*the few, the rare*) suddenly find ourselves no longer mere beings; rather the leap *which expects nothing immediate from beings, takes us into the belonging to Being in the full essential occurrence of Being as event.*[93]

---

92 Ibid., 179.
93 Ibid.

4

Dōgen's Being-Time

Like Heidegger's incipient thinking towards the in-between in the *Contributions*, Eihei Dōgen's thinking is not based solely on a "predictable" logic, nor is it a mere metaphysical speculation, but, as we have seen already with the German, relies to a great deal on both the practice of *thinking* and an equally authentic encounter with*in* a world (and not with*out* it) through the event of the disclosure of truth. One of the fundamental agreements between Heidegger and Dōgen is that both imagine that an essential fundamental discomfort of beings in the world relates to a basic, profound misconception of the question of time. From this quotidian misconception, as we have already seen with Heidegger, grows an existential crisis that relates to the limitations of metaphysical thought and the creation of a "ground" which is viewed, utterly erroneously, as solid. While the two thinkers can never, as we have already written, be entirely compared, the concept of finding an echo of one in the other remains necessary to understanding their respective positions in a deeper way. One objection to reading Heidegger through Dōgen and Dōgen through Heidegger might be that one believes fundamentally in something, while the other believes in nothing. Though Heidegger seems to feel that there is a something (*even within the quivering between, even within the abyss*), Dōgen represents, to a certain degree, the traditional Buddhist notion that everything in the universe arises, changes, dies and there is nothing that is not subject to these laws of impermanence and death; that is, there is no thing there, and this nothingness underlies al that is. Yet, both thinkers tread close to defying their own understanding; Heidegger writes again and again about nothingness while to read in Dōgen the doctrine of emptiness as a mere nihilistic negation (as Nietzsche read Buddhism) is to miss the point that each entity or phenomena is absolutely without a perduring or permanent self, that is, that emptiness goes far beyond mere nothingness.

Dōgen presents, in his fascicle "Uji" (which we will translate, with Abe and Waddell, as "being-time" though Hee-Jin Kim chooses "existence-time") an entirely unfamiliar, disquieting understanding of the way time, or being-time, presents itself, or makes itself apparent. In "Uji" we see a time that is always occurring, not as discrete separate moments, but as *all time, all the time*. This fascicle, unlike the previously examined "Genjōkōan," was written not for lay people but for monks, and Dōgen's language, as well as his choice of examples and metaphors is at times, or often, obscure and even impenetrable. Using Heidegger's imprecations as a guide, however, we must attempt to "leap" into the space of no space between thoughts, and to plumb our way into "Uji."

In a very real sense, time, or "being-time," for Dōgen, is the primordial underpinning of all phenomena, or *dharmas*; being-time is what "allows" phenomena to presence and come to be. Before going forward, it is critical that we pause to examine, if only briefly and in coarse terms, the historic time that Dōgen is thinking within, or from. As a Buddhist, Dōgen was practicing in and reacting to, certain traditions and historical events within his own lifetime, and within Buddhism itself. In this sense, he is not unlike Heidegger, who could not avoid a thinking which too often grappled — and is constrained — by the historical issues of his time. Thirteenth century Japan was, for the most part, a foreboding and corrupt place, torn apart by warring factions and corrupt landlords; the old order was withering and a new order had yet to replace it. A Mongolian invasion from the North threatened to wipe out the entire society. Like Hobbe's world come real, life was, in general, rather "nasty, brutish and short." People despaired of the world and retreated into the external and material pleasures of sensuous enjoyments. Much of this was due to a rapidly changing world and a devolution of society (in this again we can see echoes of Heidegger's own situation within the Weimar Republic, and the emerging, disastrous — yet initially attractive, to Heidegger — ideology of National Socialism.)

The sect of Buddhism[1] which exerted the most control over Dōgen's thinking, at least initially, was a philosophy practiced in China during the T'ang Dynasty (618–907 CE) called Hua-Yen. Hua-Yen philosophy, itself a syncretic school based as much on both Indian Buddhist and Hindu systems, as on native Taoist thought, describes a world of deep "interpenetration" and "non-obstructionism" of all phenomena in their relations with each other. Hua-Yen is based most closely on the conception of The Great Jewel Net of Indra which describes a vast net which at each interstice is studded with a rare, multi-faceted jewel within which is reflected, in an infinite way, each other jewel of the infinite net. Described by Francis Cook in this brief paragraph, the parable works to describe the interdependence of each phenomena within the occurrence of each other arising, or presencing, phenomena.

Far away in the heavenly abode of the great god Indra, there is a wonderful net that has been hung by some cunning artificer in such a manner that it stretches out infinitely in all directions. In accordance with the extravagant tastes of deities, the artificer has hung a single glittering jewel in each "eye" of the net, and since the net itself is infinite in all dimensions, the jewels are infinite in number. There hang the jewels, glit-

---

1   I use the term sect loosely here; unlike Western conceptions of the internecine struggles of sectarian differences, a sect in Buddhism refers more closely to a differing doctrinal opinion, and it was common, according to Francis Cook, for a Buddhist to follow one "sect" in thought and another in practice; according to Cook, the Chinese have a saying, "Hua-Yen for philosophy, Ch'an [Zen] for practice."

tering like stars of the first magnitude, a wonderful sight to behold. If we now arbitrarily select one of these jewels for inspection and look closely at it, we will discover that in its polished surface there are reflected all the other jewels in the net, infinite in number. Not only that, but each of the jewels reflected in this one jewel is also reflecting all the other jewels, so that there is an infinite reflecting process occurring.[2]

While this may seem a far-fetched descriptor, it accurately grasps the most profound aspects of Hua-Yen philosophy; all things are inter-dependent and have mutual co-origination. Each *dharma*-occurrence comes to be with and within the occurrence of each, other discrete *dharma*-occurrence, infinitely repeating itself through endless reflections and echoes. In commenting on this concept, Joan Stambaugh refers us to Leibniz's monads which reflect, through a Western interpretation, a similar idea. Stambaugh writes comparing Liebniz to Dōgen, that "every being that exists is a finite monad [... and] contains or mirrors the whole world."[3] Of course, for Dōgen, Leibniz's concern for an ultimate monad, a metaphysical "ground," is not a concern. Hee-Jin Kim,[4] also writing on Dōgen, describes the Hua-Yen process as a philosophical and religious attempt to understand the self and the world in its totality. Without giving in to essentialism, Kim writes that each *dharma*, or occurring phenomena, is infinitely formed not through a self-nature (nor does any thing abide in anything approximating a self-nature), but rather that,

---

2   Francis Cook, *Hua-Yen Buddhism; The Jewel Net of Indra* (University Park & London: The Pennsylvania University Press, 1977), 2.

3   Joan Stambaugh, *Impermanence Is Buddha-Nature: Dōgen's Understanding of Temporality* (Honolulu: University of Hawaii Press, 1990), 33.

4   While it is not my desire to draw on modern interpretations of the thinking of Heidegger and Dōgen, I prefer, as I am writing for an audience not entirely versed in Buddhist philosophy, to occasionally refer to a contemporary thinker, at least in the case of Eihei Dōgen.

[t]he entire universe consisted of creative processes in which the multiplicity of things and events interacted with and interpenetrated one another without obstruction. Particularities were not obliterated or deficient in any way, yet were unhindered in the perfect harmony of the total Dharmarealm. This non-obstruction (*muge*) was possible through the mediation of emptiness. This grand cosmic process of interaction, interpenetration, and integration in all realms, dimensions, perspectives of the self and world that went on endlessly (*jūjū-mujin*).[5]

This is a radical, almost Heraclitean way of observing the worlding of world. Nothing is permanent, everything is in flux, and, as something comes to be, it is always already reliant in its phenomenological presencing on everything else. As something comes to be, therefore, it carries with it — as a stain, or trace — everything else. Far from resting, however, in nihilistic resignation, it is precisely this flux, this movement which gives to phenomena a soteriological freedom to be, to *be*-come. In this freedom precisely lies its radicality. To recognize that no thing has a perduring essence, and indeed that each thing is a reflection of everything else, is a far cry from how ontologically we have traditionally viewed the world. To a certain extent, and Dōgen was intimately aware of this, linguistic convention is to blame for giving this artificial permanence to the world. We observe a phenomena and language requires us to name it, thereby using a term that identifies only the limited set of properties that characterize the phenomena in the same way through all points of time. Language denies the occurring flux of a dynamically changing world and replaces it with an inauthentic permanency. Viewing the entire "universe" as a vast and infinite interaction and interpenetration of all things takes us beyond language, and this is the exact point of the Hua-Yen philosophy, if not Buddhism itself; if we move beyond language to a point where we can see that things are entirely inter-manifesting in their total-

---

5   Hee-Jin Kim, *Eihei Dōgen* (Sommerville: Wisdom Publications, 2004), 145.

ity, we are no longer "claiming" things in the world for us, but "allowing" things to be as they are. We are allowing things to come to be as authentic, presencing phenomena in their own field; we no longer bend and form things to conform to our own conceptions and ideas of what world is. This standpoint, potentially, has massive implications for who and how we are in the world. If language is able to fix a point, and to give it permanency, what happens when we take away this language, the right to name? While there lies a temptation to go further into the study of Hua-Yen and its theory of interpenetration, for the purpose of this study we must restrict ourselves to Dōgen; suffice it to say, much of what Dōgen is writing to and thinking through is deeply influenced by the philosophies of Hua-Yen.

Dōgen begins "Uji" quoting extensively a long, poetical description of what "happens" in being-time. He writes:

> *An old buddha said:*
> *For the time being, I stand astride the highest mountain peaks.*
> *For the time being, I move on the deepest depths of the ocean floor.*
> *For the time being, I'm three heads and eight arms.*
> *For the time being, I'm eight feet or sixteen feet.*
> *For the time being, I'm a staff or a whisk.*
> *For the time being, I'm a pillar or a lantern.*
> *For the time being, I'm Mr. Chang or Mr. Li.*
> *For the time being, I'm the great earth and heavens above.*[6]

Each line begins with *uji*, and is as if, as Joan Stambaugh has written, someone had asked Dōgen, "What is *uji*?" Stambaugh writes that what is important here is not that things are in time, but that *they are time*. Dōgen ends the passage by declaring (and no longer in verse) that "the 'time-being' means time, just as it is, and being is all time."[7] By joining the two phrases, "be-

---

6   Eihei Dōgen, *The Heart of Dōgen's Shōbōgenzō*, trans. Norman Waddell and Masao Abe (Albany: State University of New York Press, 2002). 48.

7   Ibid.

ing" and "time" to each other, he has created a single concept which is very different from how we might imagine time to be, or even how we conceive of being. There is a long history — especially in the West — of imagining that being *becomes* within time, or that time, as a separate phenomenon, passes (or flies) by being. But, however being and time are conceived, they remain two. For Dōgen the two concepts, like Heidegger's time-space, are equiprimordial; they originate on, and as, a deeper and more profound ground than anything that rests on them. Though we might perceive them as separate categories (though tightly joined), for Dōgen, they appear, through closer examination, as a single occurrence. Thus the concepts of time and being emerge, through the conjoining of *uji,* to mean "being-time"; time becoming being and being becoming time — each exists in a mutually interpenetrated position to the other which is primordial and profound. There is no time without space, nor can there be space without time, but this does not mean to Dōgen, that one is separate from the other; they are one on a primordial level, and only come to be experienced as separate within the world of mundane reality. This is not to say that a conception of time as flying by, or as a container, or as anything separate is not categorically false, but only, for Dōgen, partial and derivative, secondary to a deeper understanding of primordial time. Dōgen is careful not to grant being and time an essential nature; like Heidegger, one can imagine the resistance that such a notion would carry for Dōgen; rather, *uji,* or being-time, emerges as the fundamental principle, always in flux, of everything that is. Whether one "is" a whisk or a pillar, Mr. Li or Mr. Chang, eight feet or sixteen feet, standing astride great peaks or at the bottom of deepest oceans, one *is* time, rather than *within* time.

It would be a mistake to imagine that what Dōgen describes in these verses are different discrete moments, as in for *this* time being, I am such and such, and for *that* time being, I am something else.[8] In the above dialectic, Dōgen is not describing a

---

8   Waddell and Abe address this concern in a footnote where they note that the characters for *u-ji* (有時) literally mean being-time but could be read

mere transformation of one thing into another, not a child into a woman, nor even a river into the sea. His description does not match up to the comfortable notions of time already discussed in Aristotle, nor do they ring true as some form of *potenza*. When time is seen as a container (as in modern physics) or even as the singular passage of one's own life (or even the "lifetime" of human history) it falls short of an actual, authentic experience of time. Dōgen is describing the presencing of time-being within all things, all apparent phenomena. Time here is not a thing but the "taking place" of all things. For Dōgen, "for the time being" refers to our prosaic, everyday experiences of time. In this instance, I am on a mountain peak, in another instance I am at the ocean, sometimes I am a pillar and other times a whisk. For most of us, these are merely the phenomena of us — *at this moment I am writing these words, later, when I have picked up my daughter, I will drive home. Yesterday I did the same thing.* Time moves in a predictable, understandable pattern, one which we can easily interpret our *self* into, a *self* that we do not have doubts about. Yet this perception of us "in" time remains inherently partial.

Continuing the fascicle, Dōgen writes that "even though you do not have doubts about them [the myriad *dharmas*], that is not to say that you know them." Like Heidegger, for the most part we never are aware of world as it "worlds" around us. World is always ready at hand and accessible as such on a certain mundane level. In our everyday selves, this is all we need world to be, but a deeper approach is existentially necessary and experienced in, for Heidegger, the crisis of the event (or equally in the *Stimmung* of boredom and anxiety.) For Dōgen, this deeper approach is found within a practice that is both profound and difficult, and which requires strong exertion (*gyoji*). We must drive ourselves towards a radical doubt (which is opposed to a mere

as *aru toki* which means "at a certain time" or "sometimes." Translated this way, *u-ji* would lend a profoundly different reading to the above quotation. Like Heidegger however, Dōgen is referring us to an older, more fundamental understanding of a term, a term that Waddell and Abe translate here as "for the time being."

acting out of doubt used by Descartes) in which the everyday mundane falls away and we experience the unglossed, unvarnished authentic nature of the world. For most "sentient beings," the "doubting of the many and various things unknown to him are naturally vague and indefinite [and] the course his doubting take will probably not bring them to coincide with this present doubt."[9] We are comfortable within our ignorance and though we claim to "know" the world, or to "know" things in it, world as such remains withdrawn and inaccessible to us. Nevertheless, writes Dōgen, "the doubts themselves are, after all, none other than time."

Dōgen presents a wholly different understanding of time than the one we have "come to know" as mundane beings in the world. Rather, he is describing a self that sets itself out (that is) atop the highest peaks and in the deepest depths of the ocean, *at the same time*; that is both eight feet and sixteen feet, that is a staff and a whisk, a pillar or lantern, *all at the same time*; the self is both Mr. Li or Mr. Chang; the self is both me and not me, you or I, *or not you or I*. The self that Dōgen describes is not the self of an immutable I or controlling ego, it is, in a Hua-Yen-istic way of thinking, a self that is all selves manifesting as all times at the same time. If we consider again the parable of Indra's jeweled net in reference to a self, we see that though there may be a self on a mundane level (*I am hungry, I am bored, I desire more*) this self is simply a self interpenetrated by world, unable to parse enough of itself to discover an original or authentic self. Dōgen writes that "we set the self out in array and make that the whole world."[10] He means here not that we discover, through introspection or practice a self that we then project, or throw, into world; rather, through the exertion (*gyoji*) of being, the self (which is not a self) is viewed as so many *dharma*-times, so many interpenetrated occasions, or even moments.

---

9   Ibid., 49.
10 Ibid.

Dōgen writes that "These things do not get in each other's way any more than various times get in each other's way."[11] Things are not substantial phenomena (they are always empty of essential nature), and this lack of inherent substantiality allows for a mutual inter-penetration of all things by all things. There is no hierarchy of times, and more importantly no individuation of discrete times; various modes of time-being cannot get in each other's way, because they are already inter-penetrated. Separating them would be like attempting to identify separate waves in the ocean. There is no clear single substance, nor are there a variety of substances; rather each thing both is (as appearing phenomena) and is not (in the sense that it does not, nor cannot, appear on its own.)

Critically important to the entire project, Dōgen is articulating a non-dual conception of time. Time is not time past or time future, nor even the Great Now, or more precisely, time is not restricted to being *only* these things (though, in an everyday sense, it seems to act like this). Time is, also *at the same time,* always arriving, occurring, and passing (though, as in Heidegger, these temporal or geographical descriptors fail us in understanding truly Dōgen's thinking). Time is always already occurring at different times *at the same time.* We come to be within time, but time is not a something — a vessel, a passage, a *thing* — within or through we which we take place. Time is as we are, and "we must see all the various things of the whole world as so many times."[12] Being *be*-comes as being-time, and not, as might be more commonly imagined, through time.

When we begin to recognize that objects have no temporal beginning nor end, we glimpse the inherent, originary emptiness of all things; we can set ourselves out as many things and see that we are not just one, and indeed are never just one. This does not mean that the self we set out is not important nor vital, only that it is not singular and unique, nor even discrete. This is not a nihilistic view of the emptiness of things, but rather its op-

11 Ibid.
12 Ibid.

posite; because each thing is Buddha-*dharma* and being-time, *all of it at the same time,* we come to recognize the infinity of all things *within their own finitude.* If no thing begins, then no thing can end. Prosaically, there is birth and death, but primordially there is no birth and death, no arising and passing — *all things simply are, as they are.* Dōgen writes:

> Since such is its fundamental reason, we must study and learn that myriad phenomena and numberless grasses [things] exists over the entire earth, and each of the grasses and each of the forms exists as the entire earth. [...] when you have arrived in this field of suchness, it is a single grass, a single form. The forms are understood and not understood, the grasses are grasped and not grasped.[13]

Each of the myriad *dharmas* appearing, or phenomena presencing themselves, are only that — an occurrence of world worlding. We deny this when we claim selfhood and permanency for ourselves and others, but this becoming is no more than the "numberless grasses" becoming. Only through study and practice do we come to recognize that, rather than individual entities standing in each other's way, each time opens (like the multi faceted jewels studding Indra's net) to another time, to each other time.

> As the time right now is all there is, each being-time is without exception the entire time. A grass being and a form-being are both times. Entire being, the entire world, exists in the time of each and every now. Just reflect: right now, is there an entire being or an entire world missing from your present time, or not?[14]

Though Dōgen writes "Uji," as we have already observed, for monks and not for lay people, he, referring to the rest of us,

---

13   Ibid.
14   Ibid., 50.

points out the common mistake that many of us make, one which is very difficult to pass beyond: that we conceive of time, when we bother to consider time at all, as passing us by, and that once past it is no longer with us. The time that many of us observe — even those of us aware of our own death — is that a single time is occurring now, and later, another time will occur. While we can conceive of times being interpenetrated, it is not ordinarily how we consider the *passage* of time; for us, on an everyday level, we pass over (or time passes us) in a predictable fashion. Thus Dōgen says, of most of us, in reading "the time being,"

> think that at one time the old Buddha became a creature with three heads and eight arms, and that at another time he became a sixteen foot Buddha. He imagines it is like crossing a river or a mountain: the river and mountain may still exists, but I have now left them behind, and at the present time I reside in a splendid vermillion palace. To him, the mountain or river and I are as distant from one another as heaven from earth.[15]

To attune ourselves to Dōgen's way of thinking, we need to be freer in the way we imagine things; our unenlightened self is stuck in a dualistic, reactionary universe in which we view ourselves and the mountain or river as somehow separate; if everything — every Buddha-*dharma* and every being-time, thus *everything as time* — exists as interpenetrated, then there can be no river and mountain left behind when I am residing in a "splendid vermillion palace." I carry with me the experiences not only of my own life, but of all times. Dōgen explains this is exactly how things occur in the world. He writes that "at the time the mountain was being climbed and the river is being crossed, I was there [in time]. The time has to be in me. Inasmuch as I am there, it cannot be that time passes away."[16] Time cannot simply

15 Ibid.
16 Ibid.

pass away (except in a prosaic way); time-being is occurring at the same time as I cross a river, or reside in a vermillion palace. In a similar fashion to the wood that *be*-comes ashes in the *Genjo-koan,* both reside in being-time, both separately and *interly.*

> The nature of the truth of this yesterday and today lies in the time when you go directly into the mountains and look at the myriad peaks around you — hence there is no passing away. […] Although it might seem as if it were somewhere else far away, it is the time right now. The sixteen foot buddha-body also makes a passage for my being-time. Although it might seem as if it were somewhere else over there, it is the time right now.[17]

If we imagine time to be flying past, we are imagining time right now, from this instant present. We cannot see the past from the past — the only way we can experience it is as right now; if we see the past, we see the past solely from the immediate now. The same holds for the future; if we imagine future times (*soon I will be residing in the vermillion palace*) it is directly informed by the immediate now (which is in turn, if only partially, informed by the reflected past and the expectant future). Mountain peaks may seem solid and permanent, but even they are simply a modality of being-time; they are *none other than time.* They are, they will always be, and yet they change. Being-time is like this; mountain peaks exist and from this moment they will always be — *in this time* — thus they are permanent. Mountains peaks exist and from this moment to the next they have changed; thus they are impermanent. What Dōgen is referring us to is precisely not a diffuse reality in which everything blends into everything else; rather, things are exactly occurring as things both in individual states (of being) and as interpenetrated (*non*)entities; things are not opposed to each other, rather they exist as being-times *within* each other.

---

17   Ibid., 51.

> The essential point is: every entire being in the entire world is each time an [independent] time, even while it makes a continuous series. Inasmuch as they are being-time, they are my being-time.[18]

Leaving aside the problematic of the excluded middle, being-times both are and they are not; one does not oppose or contradict the other but rather makes itself *both* independent and dependent. "Hence, pine trees are time. So are bamboos."[19] This is called *penetrating exhaustively.*

> To immediately manifest the the bodying of the tall golden Buddha with the body of the tall golden Buddha as the arising of the religious mind, as practice, as enlightenment, as nirvana — that is being, that is time. One does nothing nothing but penetrate exhaustively entire time as entire beings. […] [E]ven the being-time of a partial exhaustive penetration is an exhaustive penetration of a partial being-time.[20]

Dōgen describes a philosophy of practice which is far from being locked in a mere anthropological way of being. Penetrating exhaustively refers us back to the exertion (*gūjin*), or total exertion (*ippō gūjin*) of phenomena. A *dharma*-time manifesting itself fully is engaged in profound exertion not as a separate thing coming to be, but in concert with all other *dharma*-times. It exerts and comes to the fore, as Dōgen writes in the *Genjo-koan,* and "when they realize one side, the other side is in darkness."[21]

It is not just ourselves that exert the "self" into the world; if we limited our understanding to in this way, we would risk inauthentically making world merely *our* world. All things exert themselves equally in the world; so the bamboo, so the boat, so my self. Mountains and rivers as all things (times) come to be

---

18 Ibid., 50.

19 Ibid., 51.

20 Ibid., 53.

21 Ibid., 41.

in a state of exhaustive, unrestrained, unending exertion. This exertion can be seen as a presencing (of being-time), as a coming to be in the immediate now of a *dharma*-time amidst myriad *dharma*-times. Our time, effectively our being-time, is no more important (to anything or anyone but us) than any other time. The pine trees and the bamboo are engaged in the same exertion as am I. While a *dharma* reveals itself, is "illumined," the rest of the world is in darkness. This does not mean that one *dharma* is raised up while the others fall to the back in a dialectical hierarchy of being-times; rather, in the flux of everything, it is the total exertion of a single *dharma* that brings the "event" of *dharma*-being to Being. Hee-Jin Kim writes that "A dharma is never juxtaposed to others; therefore, dharmas never oppose one another in a dualistic fashion. A dharma is, by definition, that particularity which transcends all forms of dualism; it is both independent of and harmonious with all dharmas."[22] A single exerting *dharma* is necessarily, by definition, beyond the manifesting of dialectical opposites; it extends itself beyond "is" and "is not" to just be being-time.

As already noted Dōgen is speaking to monks in his fascicle, and as a result, without practice, as lay people we inevitably remain outside an entirely complete understanding of what is being said. Our exegesis will necessarily always be partial, always already lacking, and yet, with Heidegger (as with Beckett), we must try. For Dōgen, as mentioned before, practice cannot remain simply in the head — though it may, expediently, begin there. We must also sit in contemplation, in *zazen,* and only through a devoted practice can we come to the Dōgenistic realization of "mind and body falling off." We will discuss this further in another chapter, but it is essential to not forget the necessity of praxis in our understanding of Dōgen. But despite the lack of a concerted effort in practice in a contemporary thinker like Heidegger, the line of thought that Dōgen is describing is

---

22 Hee-Jin Kim, *Dōgen on Meditation and Thinking: A Reflection on His View of Zen,* (Albany: SUNY Press, 2006), 63.

not that far away from our own contemporary understanding of the event of truth.

Though the gulf between Heidegger and Dōgen may at times seem wide, it remains possible to, if not compare the two, at least to anticipate in our reading, an echo of each within each other. In his leaping forward into the abyssal beyond, Heidegger urges thinking towards the outer perimeter of thinking's boundaries, far beyond the safety net of Descartes' *cogito* (which, after methodological doubt, returned thinking to the safe and logical space of rational thought) and into a sphere of creativity which, it seems, not even Heidegger was able to "think" in its entirety. He resisted any answer, and in this sense, Heidegger was urging us towards a practice of pure thinking, far more than putting forward a system *per se.* His concern lay, as already noted, with the activity of, or towards, thinking, through the *praxis* of strength, decisiveness, mildness, and simplicity. At least in the *Contributions* Heidegger resisted describing a system more methodological than a leap towards a new beginning. Like Descartes, Heidegger's thinking throws us into uncertainty, into doubt, yet, unlike the Frenchman, resists returning us to the bourgeois safety of our chateau, pajama clad, pipe in hand.

In a similar way, Dōgen, though more systematic in his approach, destroyed an almost eight hundred year tradition of inherited and corrupted (in his eyes) Buddhist thinking through his directions toward a form of radical doubting which would have been familiar to Heidegger. Until Dōgen began teaching, Buddhism was, in many places, mired in corruption and easy answers, defining a way of belief (as opposed to doubt) that brought thinking away from the brink of nothingness and emptiness towards a complex metaphysical system which deified the idea of the Buddha (the historical personage of Siddhartha Gautama) and reserved enlightenment for those who could afford it. Dōgen's contribution to the religion was to break open the doors of what was rapidly becoming an ossified and oppositional thinking in favor of a more ambiguous, even abyssal, form of radical thought.

Not only did the two thinkers radically "destroy" the idols of rational tradition, but each engaged in a restructuring and reorienting of the grounds from which true thinking could come to be. We have so far examined the new beginning in thinking (explicit, in Heidegger, and less so in Dōgen) as well as the radically different conceptions of time. Both thinkers move in this direction with the explicit aim of persuading us to carefully think *thinking* differently; in Heidegger's case, this meant a chance to rethink the ground and to think it abyssally, while with Dōgen, we have seen that his aim was to "cast off one's body and mind and the bodies and minds of others as well."[23]

As we will see in the next chapter, the terms that Dōgen and Heidegger use can, at times, be read as not that far apart. Heidegger's the *Augenblick,* which we have so far only alluded to — that "glance of an eye" though which the presencing of the event of truth — of *Ereignis* — takes place, can be contrasted with the profound insight offered by Dōgen's treatment of *nikon,* or the absolute now. Both require an attunement that takes one away from the common, temporal understandings of time and into the primordial experience of the moment *happening,* removing it from the idea of a moment-to-moment experience.

Heidegger describes the *Augenblickstatte* as a site (*Raum*) which one enters or falls into at a given time (*Zeit*), yet it is in these moments — reserved again only *for the few, for the rare* — where the experience of truth as unconcealment is experienced through the event of appropriation. Heidegger writes that "the *site of the moment* arises out of the solitude of the great stillness in which appropriation becomes truth."[24] This moment — these moments — are approached, as we have seen, through an intimation of the nothingness of the clearing. It is within these moments, that the leap has taken place, that the

23 Dōgen, *The Heart of Dōgen's Shōbōgenzō,* 41.

24 Martin Heidegger, *Contributions to Philosophy (Of the Event),* trans. Richard Rojcewicz and Daniela Vallega-Neu (Bloomington: Indiana University Press, 2012), 255.

falling is no longer a negative, but in fact a finding, if only a finding of oneself with, and within, the abyssal *space between.*

Dōgen describes the entering of being-time, or *uji,* as a "penetrating exhaustively."[25] In their primordial "time," things — all things — are already being-time, but to attend to them, to recognize them within their ownmostness, a practice of thinking must be undertaken, a practice in which an utter penetration of each other's time (as being-time) must be embraced, and not resisted. *Hence, pine trees are time.* So are bamboos.[26] Our logical, rational world, since Aristotle, and repeated subsequently in the sciences as too obvious to question, describes a separation between pine trees and bamboo, and certainly between myself and bamboo. For Dōgen, each phenomena, while containing no essential nature, no absolute, is at the same time, inhabiting, at this moment, its ownmost time. Dōgen writes "You must not by your own maneuvering make it into nothingness; you must not force it into being."[27] Being-time is unaffected by our own "maneuvering," it exists whether or not we attend to it; enlightenment follows through observing it, allowing it to be, but not seeking to control it in any fashion whatsoever. In a similar way, the thinking that Heidegger calls and points us towards, especially as it occurs with the *Augenblickstätte,* cannot be forced; it must appropriate itself to itself in order to be authentic, in order to be itself. If you insist the bamboo to be bamboo for you, rather than imagining or allowing (Dōgen would use *seeing*) the bamboo to simply be bamboo (as well as everything else — all the myriad *dharma*) then you strip it of what it actually is — bamboo in this present time.

In the following chapter, we will examine more deeply Heidegger's *Augenblick* and Dōgen's *nikon* in an effort to bridge the large chasm which still separates the two.

---

25 Dōgen, *The Heart of Dōgen's Shōbōgenzō,* 53.

26 Ibid., 51.

27 Ibid., 53.

5

Augenblickstätte and *Nikon*

In this chapter, we will continue to look at the different (though, as already pointed out, at times, similar) ways in which Heidegger and Dōgen conceptualize thinking the idea of the timeless-time of the now-time. This thinking is of a primordial time, and if we are to think with Heidegger (and to think with Dōgen as well) it is critical to understanding the space of the event, the place of pure, undistorted, perceiving that both Heidegger and Dōgen point us towards. To open us to the event of pure perception, to ready the ground for a new beginning, to prepare us to *be*-come, Heidegger draws on a long tradition and understanding of the *Augenblick*. As with all things in Heidegger however, his contributions to understanding this concept are unique and solitary.

In *The Glance of an Eye*, William McNeil traces the attempt to think the *Augenblick* from Heidegger's understanding of it and locates its genesis in Aristotle's original five-fold description of the phenomenon of perception (*All men desire to know*[1]), described in Book I of the *Metaphysics*. Aristotle read in *theōria* the idea of "seeing" or "pure beholding"; knowing and seeing, then, are bound to each other inextricably, and perception — or, to take the argument away from the purely visual — the *perceiv-*

---

1   Aristotle, *The Works of Aristotle,* trans. W.D. Ross (Chicago: The University of Chicago, 1952).

ing of a world is to behold and know a world. In desiring to know, according to both McNeill and Heidegger, all men desire to see. In the perceiving, we open ourselves not just to the *seeing* with eyes, but to the senses which are located primordially in our experiencing, that exist *avant* our approach — not just to *listen,* but to listen to the unsaid, the unheard, the silences *in between*; to *taste* what cannot be tasted merely on the palate, but which evokes a flavor of something forgotten; to smell in a flower or a dung heap not just the most apparent smells but to the unsmelt. In this world, the *hearing,* the *smelling,* the *seeing,* the *tasting,* the *touching* are not merely hearing, smelling, seeing, tasting and touching; they are, in encountering the myriad phenomena, what defines the human being. *All men desire to know. All men desire to see.* To perceive is to come to know, and in perceiving we open ourselves to the act of knowing, or to the possibility of experiencing something we had not known, or seen before. To desire this is not simply a want or a requirement. To desire is to crave, to demand, to pull towards. That which is desired calls forth the subject to ardourosly desire. Earlier in this study we evoked Heidegger's "draft" of thinking as that which attracts us by its withdrawal; Heidegger writes that "we are who we are by pointing in that direction."[2] This desire acts as a draft towards the between of the sensed, and works to open us to a world already present, yet not yet sensed.

The *Augenblick,* as a "blink of an eye," is a sudden seeing, an unexpected illumination of a world, dark in its withdrawal. Through the *Augenblick,* this world is suddenly remembered, brought to the foreground, *en*lightened. It occurs, as the name suggests, in an instant, and, like a spark, is gone as we come to perceive it; the *Augenblick* is already in the past as it comes to be. In this way, it acts as a portal; it is not a something, but, as a vehicle, brings something to something. In its absenting, the suddenness of its departure is felt as a presence, if only an

---

2   Martin Heidegger, *Basic Writings,* ed. David Farrell Krell (New York: Harper & Row, 1977), 374.

absent presence, something wished for, with ardour, something desired.

We see flashes of the *Augenblick* throughout Western thought, especially within mystical traditions. Hegel, though far from dealing with the concept in anything close to a sustained way, seems to hint towards this idea when he discusses the "fire process" as a "flash" (*Augenblick*) which brings forth — momentarily — the distinguishing character of life. In both Kierkegaard and especially Nietzsche, concerns with the existential, transcendental moment of seeing afforded by the Augenblick are paramount. For Kierkegaard, the glance of an eye operating as a sudden, transcendental moment is called the *Øieblik* and lays the ground for a moment of revelation, the preparation for the leap out of ordinary time and the forging of a subjective experience of something "eternal" and "transcendent." In Kierkegaard, we see the existential movement of the "glance" become a transformative reordering of the self, directing experience towards a higher, more meaningful existence.[3]

For Heidegger as well, the *Augenblick* is born in a moment of existential crisis, except that this moment risks, unless surpassed, resulting in destruction and loss. The impetus for transformation — perhaps in the wake of the social and political cataclysms of the twentieth century — and its destruction, from Auschwitz to Dresden to Hiroshima, is paramount for Heidegger, and it is in crisis where we are most able, most prepared, to experience the *Augenblick.* Heidegger sees in Nietzsche a similar resonance of the crisis and he takes up this concern with a sustained reading of the "Moment" in his two volume study and lecture course on Nietzsche from 1943. Heidegger in his thinking alludes often to what the space, or clearing, of the *Augenblick* allows; that within that clearing, *Ereignis* as the authentic manifesting of *alētheia,* may take place.

---

3   Søren Kierkegaard, *The Concept of Anxiety: A Simple Psychologically Orienting Deliberation on the Dogmatic Issue of Hereditary Sin,* trans. Reidar Thomte (Princeton: Princeton University Press, 1980), 70.

For Dōgen, as a thinker from a distinctly different time and tradition, the challenge of a closely defined *Augenblick* is admittedly somewhat harder to take up and the risks in doing so are greater. We will see, however, in passages of "Uji" and elsewhere "echoes" of this concept. In Dōgen's imprecation to watch our coarse understanding of prosaic time, like body and mind, "fall away" in order to "allow" an understanding of a primordial time to manifest itself, what arises he will call the "right-now" or "here and now" of *nikon*. The experiencing of *nikon* as the exposure of oneself to the "mutual non-obstruction of things and things" is akin, perhaps, to what Heidegger refers when he describes the human being as "that which is wafted along by history (the event) and swept up into Being, that which belongs to Being."[4] Both ideas echo, closely for Heidegger and less so for Dōgen, Aristotle's conception of perception, especially as seen in the opening of *Metaphysics*.

While a direct line of thinking from Aristotle through Dōgen to Heidegger is tenuous at best, it is critical to our study to examine how we can read in each thinker's preferred terms the echoes we have sought. In *nous* for Aristotle, *satori* or *kensho* for Dōgen, and the *Augenblick* for Heidegger, there exist similarities in our experiences of them, but there are just as many limitations. Each points us to a place where language as a pointer falls away, and we are left, perhaps permanently, in the space where the sensible world we have experienced heretofore is left behind. Like Wittgenstein, we are left at a place where language can no longer serve us. For Aristotle, *nous* came to mean, as the five of the highest virtues of thinking, a sort of unmediated intellectual apprehension of *phainomena*. We place ourselves in a wondering relation to the world, and, at a certain point, after the practices of the other forms of cognition are mastered, we avail ourselves of the pure apprehending of a world. In Dōgen, it is the experience of *satori*, or *kensho*, that is a priority. It is important to note

---

4   Martin Heidegger, *Contributions to Philosophy (Of the Event)*, trans. Richard Rojcewicz and Daniela Vallega-Neu (Bloomington: Indiana University Press, 2012), 387.

that though *satori* is often translated as enlightenment, it means, more closely, "momentary awareness." Though often used interchangeably, *kenshō* is translated most closely as meaning "seeing onto one's own nature." Whichever term is used, the process of exposure to the emptiness of all things is the critical goal of Zen practice, and is best described by the phrase already used by Dōgen, that of "body and mind falling off." These two concepts — the unmediated experience of *phainomena* in Aristotle and the pure seeing of emptiness in the Zen tradition — ready us to understand more clearly the *Augenblick,* or "sudden glance of the eye" through which our most transitory, finite selves are revealed in an equally finite world.

As already noted, to describe a one-to-one comparison with *nous* and Dōgen's experience of time is flawed, as flawed perhaps as comparing *nous* directly with *Augenblick*. And yet can we not hear an echo of one in the other? In the Aristotelian experience of pure apprehending, of, colloquially, "getting it," there is a movement of the falling away, the dropping-off of imposed and artificial separation between phenomena, between me and it, that takes place. This falling away into pure perception has not been taken seriously often enough, the challenge has not been taken up in the West; the claim to our inability, via Kant, to experience the noumenal world has been taken ipso facto. According to Kant's theory of transcendental idealism, we are permanently removed — estranged — from the world "as it is." Our intuition is limited to perceiving mere representations of appearances, and never things as they are in themselves. Through reading with others, with Heidegger, with Dōgen, we can begin to understand this space between which Heidegger describes, the clearing between, the abyssal which opens constantly. And with Dōgen's "total exertion" or *gujin* we see a reference to the undefiled freedom and liberation of the self (and thereby the world) that takes place in the noumenal apperception of world. Can we not understand, more clearly, both the concept of *nikon,* that immediate here and now of pure perceiving which Dōgen describes, and *nous,* the un-rendered beyond of Aristotle, and thereby *Augenblick,* through reading them side by side by side?

Can we not indeed hear or see a trace, a Derridean specter or even stain of an idea, in the three? And if we can hear, should we not then listen?

A Blink of an Eye

The *Augenblick* at its most basic refers to a "blink" or a "glance of an eye." As a metaphor, it refers to the sudden awareness, a total seeing or perception through which one transcends one's own reality or world for a world unencumbered by subjectivities and prosaic, quotidian concerns; it allows one suddenly, temporally, to see the world "as it is," bounded in a finite infinitude. Yet this transcension operates not by removing one to an other world; rather the *Augenblick* reveals the world as it, as an authentic coming to be. It describes a moment of fleeting suddenness, an awareness of what has already passed, and what is gone as it is coming to be. At the same time, a portal to an other experience of reality — the evental experience of truth — is, in accordance with the very nature of the human being, caught as we are in the web of a finite, lived experience of world — gone in, quite literally, an "instant." Though gone, the direct experience of the *Augenblick* results in an altered perception of one's own time; the experience seems to make time *stand out of time,* to be bounded by an authentic experience of the limitless horizon of a state of possibility. The experience of the *Augenblick* serves to clear away the dross of the world, clearing the clearing for the evental experience of truth.

The *Augenblick* can be compared (and indeed is not dissimilar) to the experience of *kaironic* time, that unique opening, or presenting of a "moment" in time in which the event of opening opens itself. As discussed in the previous chapter, this thinking of time is not unique to an understanding of the *Augenblick,* but it is, at least from the perspective of the West, effective tool for gaining insight into how time manifests differently; the *Augenblick* presents itself to the present time as an encountering. This encountering is a waiting-towards similar to Boethius's conception of *nunc stans,* of "standing now." Heidegger writes that nothing happens in the *Augenblick,* that what happens is an encountering, or "waiting-towards," possibility. In *Being and Time,* Heidegger writes:

> The presence [*Gegenwart*] which is held in temporality and which is thus authentic, we call the *Augenblick.* This term must be understood in the active sense as an ecstasis. It means the rapture of resolute openness in which Dasein is carried away towards whatever possibilities and circumstances are encountered in the situation, but a rapture that is held in this resolute openness. The *Augenblick* is a phenomenon that in principle can not be clarified in terms of the "now." The "now" is a temporal phenomenon that belongs to time as within-time-ness: the "now" "within which" something arises, passes away, or is present-at-hand. Nothing can occur in the *Augenblick*; rather, as authentic presence or waiting-toward [*Gegen-wart*], the *Augenblick* lets us first encounter whatever can be "in a time" as ready-to-hand or present-to-hand.[5]

Whichever concept we choose to align ourselves with, what is clear is that the *Augenblick* is a radical departure — a new possible beginning — in how we conceive time, and thereby in how we ready ourselves to anticipate being. For most of our lives, time is a series of now-events; a rapidly dissolving line of present moments which dissipate into a miasma of memory (and in which, if I am to distinguish, or remember, a present moment, I am always bound from this moment to conceive of a moment in the past.) Time stretches distantly into both a futural not yet now and a past just gone. The *Augenblick,* as a single moment, as a singular glance of an eye, is used by Heidegger, and by Nietzsche before him, as a distinctly atemporal disruption in the unending linearity of prosaic time; the *Augenblick* is a sudden irruption which alters everything whilst everything, within its

---

5   Martin Heidegger, *Being and Time,* trans. John Macquarrie and Edward Robinson (New York: Harper & Row, 1962), 338.

quotidian, prosaic reality, remains the same; present moments pass, the sun still sets, the shadows lengthen (for Dōgen, weeds grow and flowers fall), yet everything, via the *Augenblick,* becomes itself primordially, comes to itself in its originary form and without distortion. It is not time itself that is changed by the experience of the *Augenblick,* time remains as time is. Rather it is the experience of time as undergone by the perceiving agent that is changed. The *Augenblick* presents itself as a moment when the moment of this moment dissolves into all time, all possibility, becoming not time as we conceive it, but time without timepieces, without timekeeping. This encounter takes us from the homogenized satiety of prosaic time to a time which is originary, primordial, and ultimately transformative, sometimes violently so. As Heidegger describes it, this encountering is an encountering of "whatever can be."

Heidegger's Zarathustra

This transformation is described when Heidegger takes up Nietzsche's treatment of the *Augenblick* in his lecture course on the thinker from the early 1940s. In Volume II of the collection, *The Eternal Recurrence of the Same,* Heidegger describes the third part of Nietzsche's *Thus Spake Zarathustra* entitled "On the Vision and the Riddle." Here Heidegger relates Zarathustra's own tale to the sailors of his ascent of the mountain, struggling as he goes with the dwarf upon his back. Early on in the lecture, Heidegger takes up the question of the title — "why a 'riddle?'" he asks. Drawing a distinction between an interpretation of the riddle as "calculation," which can only "disclose step by step [...] something unknown from what is known,"[6] or as "surmise," which for Heidegger involves inevitably "a leap, without guidelines, without the rungs of any ladder which anyone can clamber up anytime," Heidegger invites us, yet again, to "ven-

---

6   Martin Heidegger, *Nietzsche Volume II: The Eternal Recurrence of the Same,* trans. David Farrell Krell (New York: Harper & Row, 1984), 37.

ture [...] into that untraveled and uncharted region which is the unconcealment (*alētheia*) of what is most concealed."[7]

The uncharted region here is Zarathustra's and describes his struggle up a mountain all the while carrying — inexplicably — a dwarf upon his back, one who threatens to drag him back down. Heidegger describes the abyss from which Zarathustra climbs that is formed by his ascension, as the "depths [which] belong to the heights."[8] In a double articulation of the described space, Zarathustra is both climbing from the abyss as he creates it through his upward movement, as well as climbing towards a peak; the ascension — like any movement — is both a from and a towards.[9] Through a withdrawal from the abyss, the valley below grows larger. "Inasmuch as Zarathustra thinks the abyss, the thought of thoughts, inasmuch as he takes the depths seriously, he rises to the heights and surpasses the dwarf."[10] As they climb, they come across a gateway, a gateway which divides two long paths (*Holzweg*). One leads forward and the other back, and both extend for "an eternity." Nietzsche writes that "they contradict each other, these paths; they offend each other face to face; and it is here at this gateway that they come together." The gateway is the "Moment" (*Augenblick*) and it is from the Moment that time runs away from us as "eternity." But here Zarathustra queries the dwarf, asking if "these paths contradict each other eternally?" and the dwarf, responding contemptuously in Nietzsche's telling, says, too easily, "Everything straight deceives [...] all truth is curved; time itself is a circle." The riddle, it would seem, is solved, and, according to Heidegger, would appear to

---

7   Reading Heidegger on Nietzsche (who is writing about Zarathustra who is recounting a tale to the sailors) extends beyond the text this *mise-en-abyme* experience. To write further about Heidegger on this includes me suddenly in this event.

8   Heidegger, *Nietzsche II,* 40.

9   One can almost hear Pessoa here, when he, writing as Bernardo Soares, writes, in *The Book of Disquiet,* "We are two abysses — a well staring at the sky" (Fernando Pessoa, *The Book of Disquiet,* trans. Richard Zenith [New York: Penguin Classics, 2002], 20).

10 Heidegger, *Nietzsche II,* 40.

be one "scarcely […] worth talking about."[11] The concept is simple — too simple really — as what looks like two straight paths inevitably leading away from one another are in reality two segments of a vast circle, "which perpetually revolves back upon itself.[12]" Yet this simplicity is deceiving, both for Nietzsche via Zarathustra and certainly for Heidegger. Zarathustra, speaking "wrathfully" curses the dwarf, calling him "lamefoot," for having simplified, too quickly, the question which is the thought of thoughts, for having reduced the question to a mere "ditty." Zarathustra immediately questions the dwarf again, correcting him. "'Behold,' I continued, 'this moment!'" From the gateway, a long path does indeed lead backwards, into an eternity. Zarathustra asks:

> Must not whatever can walk have walked on this lane before? Must not whatever can happen have happened, have been done, have passed by before? And if everything has been there before […] must not this gateway have been there before? And are not all things knotted together so firmly that this moment draws after it all that is to come? therefore — itself too?[13]

While this thought of the eternal recurrence of the same has within it the potential for the familiar nihilistic disinterestedness of the dwarf's response, it is, for Heidegger, specifically *that* command of Zarathustra's — "Behold this Moment!" where the leap is made. The beholding of the Moment is a connection to authentic world, to a perduration of attention which leads one into the clearing. The boldness of that leap is precisely what differentiates Zarathustra from the dwarfish thoughts of others. If everything that must have happened has happened, then it is within the gateway of the Moment (*Augenblick*) that

---

11   Ibid., 42.

12   Ibid.

13   Friedrich Nietzsche, *Thus Spake Zarathustra,* trans. R.J. Hollingsdale (London: Penguin Books, 1969), 179.

the "moment" of decision is made; all is not lost to disinterest-
ed nihilism — indeed the opposite occurs; within the event of
the *Augenblick,* within what Heidegger will refer to elsewhere
as the *Augenblickstätte,* the site of the *Augenblick,* authenticity
as *alētheia* appears, is appropriated and is made its own. Truth
events — *be-*comes — in the site of the moment, and the dwarf
as the little man disappears, leaving one "suddenly alone, bleak,
in the bleakest moonlight."[14]

> After Zarathustra has posed the second [command] there is
> no place left for the dwarf, who no longer belongs in the realm
> of this question because he cannot bear to hear it. Question-
> ing, riddling and thinking, as they approach ever nearer the
> import of the riddle, themselves become more riddlesome,
> loom ever more gigantic, towering over the one who is doing
> the questioning. Not everyone has a right to every question.
> Rather than expect a response from the dwarf, and rather
> than reply a polished reply couched in propositions, Zara-
> thustra continues the narrative: "Thus I spoke, and ever more
> softly: for I feared my own thoughts and hinterthoughts."
> The thought that is hardest to bear grows terrifying. Behind
> what one may imagine as a turning in lazy circle, it decries
> something altogether different. It thinks the thought in a way
> dwarfs never think it.[15]

For Heidegger, that awareness of the Augenblick, that experiencing of the site of truth, is what differentiates our thought (*if
we are to think*) from that of "the little man." He writes that,
"precisely, the knowledge that chokes us is what must be known
if being as a whole is to be thought,"[16] and that this thinking
marks the "altogether unbridgeable difference between the usual kinds of spectation and cognition…and proper knowing."[17]

---

14 Ibid.
15 Heidegger, *Nietzsche II,* 44.
16 Ibid., 55.
17 Ibid.

The problem that remains unacknowledged when we do not avail ourselves, or present ourselves to the evental moment, the problem when we treat the riddle as contemptuous, when we remain, out of fear, out of derision, on the periphery, like the dwarf, is that we allow being to hide, occluded within the negative, and destroyed within nihilism. Heidegger writes that what allows the doctrine (or eternal recurrence) to be turned into a mere ditty is that

> the latter concedes that things do depart, die, and disintegrate; it also accepts everything negative, adverse, and outrageous. Yet at the bottom these things are conceived of as eventually passing away in the world's circuitry, so that other things will come and everything shall take a turn for the better. Hence all is bound for perpetual compensation. Such compensation in fact makes everything indifferent: striving is flattened out into mere alternation. One now possesses a handy formula for the whole and abstains from all decision.[18]

This abstention denies us being, denies being the encounter with Being, for "to see the Moment means to stand in it. But the dwarf keeps to the outside, perches on the periphery"[19] where it is safest, but where one is consequently condemned to the petty, to the small. It is by availing oneself to the darkest thoughts, the thoughts still to be thought, that being advances to Being. This is "what is hardest to bear." Heidegger continues,

That which is to come is precisely a matter of decision, since the ring is not closed in some remote infinity but possesses its unbroken closure in the Moment, as the center of the striving: what recurs — if it is to recur — is decided by the Moment and by the force with which the Moment can cope with whatever in it is repelled by such striving.[20]

---

18 Ibid., 56.
19 Ibid., 57.
20 Ibid.

The decision then of the Moment, of the *Augenblick,* is powerfully within the grasp of the one who is grasping, the one who is striving. It is for the being who has prepared for the encounter, who has trained and readied herself for the struggle, for she who has practiced most arduously.

> That is what is peculiar to, and hardest to bear in, the doctrine of the eternal return — to wit, that eternity is the Moment, that the Moment is not the fleeting "now," not an instant of time whizzing by the spectator, but the collision of future and past. Here the Moment comes to itself. It determines how everything recurs. Now the most difficult matter is the most tremendous matter to be grasped, and the tremendous remains a sealed door to little men.[21]

The *Augenblick* then becomes, rather than a mere waypoint through which pass the times of future and past, a gateway which is the site of the momentous event of being as Being and for truth, as unconcealment, to come forth, whereby the appropriating event takes place. It is not a clash, nor even a gateway as such; to experience the *Augenblick* is to be the *Augenblick.* It is not to be remaindered as a peripheral force but to be the force itself, to be energy manifesting itself as such; not to be the bystander sitting upon a stump looking on, but rather to be looking from within. This is what, for Nietzsche, as for Heidegger is meant by the thinking of the most abyssal thought. The person who can think this way can

> also overcome his outrage and repugnance by learning that the abyss belongs to the heights. To overcome outrage is not to put it out of action but to acknowledge its necessity. As long as outrage is merely repudiated by disgust, as long as our contempt is determined by Nausea, that contempt remains dependent upon the contemptible. Only when contempt springs from love of the task, being transformed in

---

21   Ibid.

such a way that, undergirded by an affirmation of the necessity of outrage, suffering, and destruction, it can pass by in silence; only when the silence of such loving passing-by prevails; only then does the vast stillness extend and the sphere expand about the one who in this way has become himself. Only now that the vast stillness pervades Zarathustra's spirit has he found his loneliest loneliness, a solitude that has nothing to do with a merely peripheral existence.[22]

It is through this movement which occurs within the moment of the *Augenblick,* which Heidegger will eventually call the event, as it occurs within the *Augenblickstätte.*

I admit to struggling with the story of the eternal recurrence of the same; it is too fanciful, too incredible — I am the "dwarf" as much as I deny it, understanding it too, too simply. And yet, and yet? Whether I understand it or not is precisely not the point — the point is the leap, the falling into the abyss, the willingness to leap, the willingness to think within the abyssal ground of the event. There is in the story, in the parable, if we allow it to be, if we open ourselves to it, a remarkable sudden pause, a falling away. What if it is true? What if we consider it not as poetry and metaphor but as possibility, seriously? What if "this slow spider, which crawls in the moonlight, and this moonlight itself, and I and you in the gateway, whispering together, whispering of eternal things — must not all have been here before?"[23] Germinating in that frightening concept lies the reason Zarathustra speaks now more and more softly and becomes afraid of his thoughts, "and the thoughts behind [my] thoughts"; the *Augenblick* here acts as a sudden portal, an opening into timeless time, into primordial time, into a new beginning. It is the falling away of body and mind, a powerful, transformative, horrifying force which takes us away, suddenly, as in a leap, from all that is known and leads us towards that new beginning.

---

22 Ibid., 60.
23 Nietzsche, *Thus Spake Zarathustra,* 180.

Dōgen's Buddha-Nature and Nikon

This portal through which Heidegger, via Zarathustra, would have us fall, or descend, or ascend, leap or be pushed, is, as just mentioned, a falling away of body and mind, a dissolution of the false duality of perceiver and receiver. It is a transition away from dialectics, a traversal *towards* another beginning. Dōgen, as quoted above, refers to a similar falling away in the "Genjōkōan" fascicle when he writes "to be confirmed by all dharmas is to cast off one's body and mind and the bodies and minds of other as well."[24] For Heidegger, it is a "venture" which "jettisons and leaves behind everything conventional"[25] and this feeling of vertigo which is elicited when the concept — if truly thought (*when we have begun to think*) — is echoed in, or echoes, at least in part, again, Dōgen's remarkable "Busshō" (Buddha-nature) fascicle, a radical, non-dualistic description of the inherent Buddha-nature which resides in all sentient beings. Like Heidegger, Dōgen (to the frustration of many a translator) rediscovered in language hidden meanings — this time in classical Chinese as opposed to the Greek — bending, and at times even torturing meaning, to fit his understanding of a concept. Like Heidegger, he does this to direct attention away from a common, prosaic reading, a reading received and accepted by *das Man* and to accent the unique, particular form of interpretation his thinking demands. In doing so, again like Heidegger, Dōgen "allows" for a clearing to take place in which understanding, as *kensho*, or pure perceiving, takes place.

Dōgen begins the "Busshō" fascicle with a quotation from the *Nirvana Sutra*, which, when translated, according to Waddell and Abe, "normally," reads "All sentient beings have the Buddha-nature." Dōgen, however, chooses to interpret the phrase to mean "All beings/entire being *is* the Buddha-nature," by, again according to Waddell and Abe, "arbitrarily reading the

---

24 Eihei Dōgen, *The Heart of Dōgen's Shōbōgenzō*, trans. Norman Waddell and Masao Abe (Albany: State University of New York Press, 2002). 41.

25 Heidegger, *Contributions to Philosophy (Of the Event)*, 179.

characters *shitsuu* [...] as 'entire being.'"[26] This interpretation has the effect of changing the meaning, and thereby the direction of our common understanding that sentient beings have an awakened awareness (of Buddha-nature) in which they have the potential to reach in some undetermined future to the more radical conception of being, as the totality of all being which is always already Buddha-nature, in the immediate now. This shift is as radical a move as Heidegger's description of the event as a clearing, or a lightening; what already is, is already there — our task is to perceive the event purely, without the mediation of an inauthentic world. We are to perceive the clearing, to allow it to unfold as it is, and not to await it in some distant yet too manifest future, not to attend it.

To Waddell and Abe, this obviates the false dichotomy of "a duality of subject (sentient beings) and object (Buddha-nature)" as they explain in a footnote to their translation of "Busshō." It serves to sever the uncomfortable idea that enlightenment (for us, awareness of world worlding) is something that comes in the future, that remains a possibility, however vague, to be replaced with a clear conception that entire being is already enlightened awareness, that the distant possibility of a futural event is already, indeed is, now in the immediate moment (as it is for all future nows). World worlding is no longer a distant concept not yet arrived; rather, being as being is now, in the particular momentless moment. Dōgen writes:

> You must understand that the "being" that the Buddha-nature makes *entire being* is not the being of being and nonbeing. *Entire being* is a Buddha's words, a Buddha's tongue, the pupils of a Buddha-patriarch's eyes, the noseholes of a Zen monk. Nor does the term *entire being* mean emergent being, or original being, or mysterious being, or anything of the like, much less conditioned being or illusory being. It has

---

26 Dōgen, *The Heart of Dōgen's Shōbōgenzō*, 60n.

nothing to do with such things as mind and object, substance and form.[27]

The being that Dōgen is describing here is simply being — not original nor primordial — it simply is being *qua* being which resides as itself, as everything that there is. Thus, for Dōgen, the mountains which are quietly walking towards the sea, indeed, are the sea by ontological necessity, as the mountains are, already, the noseholes of a Zen monk. This is not to say that everything just is everything else; that view would leave us in an amorphous bog of being and becoming. Rather, everything has, immanently, everything else, and therefor is, in some reading of it, everything else. There is no futural being to which some one or any thing aspires, and the teleological arc of temporal domains is done away with. Entire being is not an imagined future, a something to become, but an ontological fact in itself, in this present time, in all present times.

No thing, however, and this is critical, is not a negation of thingness. In traditional Western metaphysics, the concept of nothing, or no thing, is nihilistic and destructive; that there is something is of importance, and no thing is a rational impossibility. But we are not discussing traditions here, and the question of whether there is something or nothing is meaningless when we attune ourselves to the possibility of a new beginning in which the dichotomy of the excluded middle is set to the side as a flawed, unhelpful, and even erroneous concept. For a thinker who is willing to think differently, who is willing, with Heidegger, to think a new beginning (who is willing to begin to think), no thing becomes, in its no-thingness, the very possibility not only of some thing but of every thing. Everything hinges on the possibility of nothingness, and of the inherent emptiness of that everything. *Nirvāṇa* in the original Sanskrit means "no wind," or "no breath," and is occasionally read as "blown out." As a concept not unlike a *via negativa* (that is, *that what is, is not that*), this negation of something refers to the perfect stillness of

---

27   Ibid., 62.

not grasping, not insisting. Instead, *nirvāṇa* points us towards an absolute emptiness as an attunement towards a reality empty of essential essence.

That everything already is, and yet is not, radically denies personal possession. No thing can be held as individual, as absolute in a world in which time, as a future predictor of emergence, is not anymore a characteristic of time as such; time is seen instead as the momentary absolute. Instead of beings in the future emerging, time is emerging for them, at this very instant. Dōgen writes that to view "the entire world and everything in it" as my personal possessions is a "false, non-Buddhist teaching." For Dōgen, entire being

> is not original (timeless) being, because it fills the past right on up through the present. It is not separate, individual beings, because it is an all-inclusive whole. It is not beginningless being, because, "What is this that thus comes." It is not being that appears at a certain time, because "my everyday mind is in the Way." You must know with certainty that with *entire being* it is impossible, even with the greatest swiftness, to encounter sentient beings. Understood in this way, *entire being* is in itself completely and totally emancipated suchness.[28]

It is important that we pause here to try and unpack this enigmatic passage. The move Dōgen is making in effect decimates our prosaic understanding of subject and object, of perceiver and perceived, of being in the world. Entire being fills time, overflows time; there is no separation between past and future, not even in the form of the present. Entire being does not begin, nor does it end in any understandable sense; it simply is, and it perdures, but not merely as a moment which passes from the future to the past in a form of exchange, but as absolute time, as, for Dōgen, "totally emancipated suchness." There is no form as time for entire being to "be"; rather entire being is, and is

---

28 Ibid., 63.

time as well. An everyday understanding of sentient beings is that they are rooted in an everyday time — things die and are born (and if we follow a Buddhist ontology, die and are born endlessly) — but entire being cannot "encounter" them, as it is wholly "suchness" and nothing else.

As a result of entire being encompassing everything, there is no thing that is not Buddha-nature, that is not already suchness as such and which has not already "filled in" everything, though even here, to use a word such as "already" denotes that there might have been a time, now past, when "already" had not yet happened. That is incorrect. We must be careful to delineate between what, for us in the West we would see as a negation, and what Dōgen views as the "no" (*mu*) in no-Buddha-nature. For Dōgen, "emptiness is not 'no'"; instead, emptiness resists the negative, and further it is emptiness precisely which allows for it, not only the possibility to be everything but also that in everything, it remains a possibility. Dōgen views *mu* as the not-that which always resists the *that*.

> Hence every piece of *mu* is a touchstone to articulate emptiness; emptiness is the capacity to articulate mu. This is not the emptiness of "form is emptiness." "Form is emptiness" does not mean form is forced into emptiness, nor is it making form out of emptiness. It has to be the emptiness of "emptiness is emptiness." The emptiness of "emptiness is emptiness" is a piece of rock in emptiness.[29]

As *mu* resists the designation of the *that*, it always already exceeds any definition of no-thingness. Nothing, then, is not the replacement of something; nothingness as emptiness remains everything while being no particular, unique thing. Emptiness allows *mu* to become no, it is the action of no, and as no, *mu* stubbornly remains a touchstone through which we interrogate and experience emptiness. To say something is merely empty is to reveal a nihilistic claim; to describe the emptiness of empti-

---

29 Ibid., 72.

ness is emptiness is to travel a far deeper route into the heart of everything's essential, inherent emptiness. This is not a forced march into nihilism, as the critics of Buddhism often claim; rather, there is at work a surrender (of one's self, one's claim to the world, one's personal and unique access the world) born out of practice, or out of attunement. Dōgen, in the "Uji" fascicle on time, advises that "You must not by your own maneuvering make it into nothingness; you must not force it into being."[30] Instead of pushing into a proof as a scientific, rational mind might insist, there is a stepping away, a stepping back to allow emptiness itself to come forward.

It is important to remember that Dōgen is not describing anything like a surrender in the "stepping away" described earlier. He uses, repeatedly through the Shōbōgenzō, two words which mean similar, though separate things; *gūjin* refers to "total exertion" and *gyōji* to "continuous practice." One cannot exist without the other, but when they are practiced, sustained, and, importantly, lived, they become powerful tools for inhabiting one's world (or via Dōgen, allowing world to inhabit one's self). Indeed, through exertion and practice, Dōgen calls on one to place oneself in the world, "to set the self out in array and make that the whole world." By setting the self out, through "total exertion," we presence ourselves in the world, and world presences through us; we become world. But this is not the ego that I put forward, the ego which insists on world. Rather, through active surrender, (and in this we can anticipate Heidegger's concept of *Gelassenheit*) we come to world in an authentic and unstained way. Dōgen writes, in the "Genjōkōan" fascicle:

> Life is, for example, like a man sailing in a boat. Although he sets sail, steers his course, and poles his boat along, the boat carries him and he does not exist apart from the boat. By sailing in the boat, he makes it what the boat is. Study assiduously this very time.[31]

---

30 Ibid.

31 Ibid.

The boat and the man are one, and though the man makes choices, decides when to leave and where to go to, and remains nominally in charge, the man does not exist as separate from the boat.[32] The man makes the boat (without him there would be no boat, or at least no 'boat function'), but the man cannot exist (in this "very time") without the boat. The man and the boat are one, and thus the dichotomies of subject and object fall away. Dōgen continues:

> At such a time, there is nothing but the world of the boat. The heavens, the water, and the shore — all become the boat's time, and they are not the same as the time that is not the boat. Hence, I make life what it is; life makes me what I am.[33]

I am not separate from what life is, though by living, I make life what life is. The heavens and the water and the boat are not separate; each thing, as am I, are exactly balanced in this very time, in this very moment. Every thing is where it should be because it can't be somewhere else.

In sailing the boat, one's body and mind, the self and the world, are together the dynamic function of the boat. The entire earth and the whole empty sky are in company with the boat's vigorous exertion. Such is the I that is life, the life that is I.[34]

Total exertion is the absolute presencing of one's self in one's activity. This could best be described as a musician performing; the total dedication that it takes for Pablo Casals or Mitsuko Uchida to present themselves to the music, and to presence the music through their "total exertion" is clear to us. For Heidegger, a similar concept is called for in relation to the cabinet maker in "What Calls for Thinking." The cabinet maker requires "relatedness" to avoid reducing his craft down to mere "busywork." The

---

32 I follow here, very roughly, Heidegger translator Joan Stambaugh's own argument on the same passage that she writes about in *Impermanence Is Buddha-Nature: Dōgen's Understanding of Temporality* (Honolulu: University of Hawaii Press, 1990), 31.

33 Dōgen, *The Heart of Dōgen's Shōbōgenzō*, 42.

34 Ibid., 42.

cabinet maker must "answer and respond above all" to the calling of the wood, "to the shapes slumbering within wood — to wood as it enters into man's dwelling with all the hidden riches of its essence."[35] In a similar fashion, the shoes in Van Gogh's painting, which are not beings as such, exert themselves according to Heidegger. In "The Origin of the Work of Art," Heidegger writes that "the more simply and essentially the shoes are engrossed in their essence, the more directly and engagingly do all beings attain a greater degree of being along with them." The more a some thing engages in its ownmost exertion of being, the more deeply does it make its presence known, even to itself. For Dōgen however, it goes much farther than a "mere" master performing a masterful work. At the risk of giving a vitalist reading to the text, Dōgen argues for every thing in the world exerting itself in its own time. The boat and the empty sky are exerting themselves as is the sailor. A flower is exerting its presence in a meadow, as is the meadow, as is the mountain towering above, as am I making my way across a valley (on which the meadow and the flower and the mountain are already also exerting). I remain, like the sailor in a boat, entities inseparable from each other, from the sky above, from the sea, both a single entity walking across a meadow and yet also utterly interconnected, even interpenetrated, by the myriad things of the world. I exert myself and sustain and perdure as something which I could not produce by myself alone, which is world. Through my exertion, I bring forth an equally exerting world.

This is admittedly hard to see, and for Dōgen, it is only through the second term mentioned above, *gyōji*, or continuous practice that we can come to experience the total exertion of world(s). Even though exertions happen constantly and we are unaware of them (the world is exerting itself now, and now, and now…) it is only through our attunement to the "myriad dharmas" that we come to be aware of it. This is different from Aristotle's sense of *potenza* which occurs in each thing; rather, in *gūjin,* or total exertion, the world is presencing itself at every

---

35 Heidegger, *Basic Writings,* 379.

moment, in this very moment. The table makes itself manifest in a very direct way, through strenuous exertion, as a table before me. The rock on the hillside behind me is manifesting itself through its own exertions, as is the ice is that is breaking up in the bay, as is the bird over head, as is my coffee in front of me, or my mobile beside me. This attunement to the presence of each thing, unique and interconnected, but vital and necessary, even to those of us who cannot see the connection, is essential to understanding the version of Buddhism that Dōgen puts forward. Continuous practice, as unremitting attunement, to a world exerting, is necessary to enter into this world which is always already present, only withdrawn, separate.

While we may talk of self as the closest thing we know, for Dōgen, the self is only that; the nearest manifestation of the myriad dharmas *be*-coming. Indeed, there are many selves, infinite selves, constantly exerting, constantly presencing. Of all the enigmas presented in the "Genjōkōan," perhaps none is as elusive as the paragraph that begins "To learn the Buddha Way is to learn one's self." Dōgen writes:

> To learn the Buddha Way is to learn one's self. To learn one's self is to forget one's self. To forget oneself is to be confirmed by all dharmas. To be confirmed by all dharmas is to cast off one's body and mind and the bodies and minds of others as well. All trace of enlightenment disappears, and this traceless enlightenment continues without end.[36]

Within traditional Western metaphysics, this self might mean the one that's found through a deep, authentic search, one that we can find, deeply within, and which remains constant. For Dōgen, it is not so easy. The self is only all selves, and it is only by practicing continuously that we come to understand this. Without continuous practice, we remain locked in the prosaic world of individual essences competing and clashing. "To forget oneself is to be confirmed by all dharmas." Only by actively leav-

---

36 Ibid., 41.

ing the self behind, the ego self that I so strenuously prioritize on a quotidian, minute-by-minute basis, can I free myself from the dichotomies of everyday existence. Only by doing this, by "allowing"[37] myself to be confirmed, am I able to "cast off [my] body and mind and the bodies and minds of others as well." This is what it means — to Dōgen — to be authentic; it means to not be the self, and to not be the self of others. The dharma is not found externally, nor is it found internally; one is inseparable from the dharma, and the dharma inseparable from one. It is only by pushing aside false views, by "allowing" (see footnote above) one's self to awaken to what is already there does one come to one's true self (which is not a self at all). Dōgen describes this process elsewhere as "the right transmission from oneself to oneself" and calls this becoming a becoming aware, or awakened to "the Person of your original part."

Joan Stambaugh, mentioned above, attempts to explain *gyūjin* through Leibniz's monads in her *Impermanence Is Buddha-Nature*. Describing a colleague who, when he could not remember the precise term Leibniz had written, used instead the word "worldlets." In Leibniz's theory, each being exists as a finite monad, a little worldlet. Each worldlet contains within itself the entire world which it mirrors, but only ever in an imprecise and partial way. For Leibniz, only God can reflect an entire world as something complete. Because of our own limitations, and the limitations of individual beings, we cannot know a monad completely; if we could, we could know the entire universe because "each monad would be a deity."[38] But, according to Leibniz, while monads are limited, they are also reaching out "in a confused way [...] to infinity or to the whole."[39] As unique, individual worldlets — worlds to themselves — monads are also

---

37 Language again begins to fail us because by "allowing" something I already admit, indeed insist, to some control over the world, when in fact I am powerless. Remember that the first paragraph of the "Genjōkōan" ends with the phrase: "Yet for all that, flowers fall amidst our regret and yearning, and hated weeds grow apace" (Dōgen, *The Heart of Dōgen's Shōbōgenzō*, 40).

38 Stambaugh, *Impermanence Is Buddha-Nature*, 33.

39 Ibid.

interconnected; each reflects the other. Each monad fills and extends itself into the world. Leibniz explains that

> composites are like simple substances, for all space is filled up; therefore, all matter is connected. And in a plenum or a filled space, every movement has an effect upon bodies in proportion to this distance, so that not only is every body affected by those which are in contact with it and responds in some way to whatever happens to them, but also by means of them the body responds to those bodies adjoining them, and their intercommunication reaches to any distance. Consequently every body responds to all that happens in the universe. Consequently every body responds to all that happens in the universe, so he who saw all could read in each one what is happening everywhere, and even what has happened and what will happen. He can discover in the present what is distant both as regards space and as regards time.[40]

While Stambaugh uses the above passage to unfold the fascicle "Uji," we can also find in it a better understanding of what Dōgen means in his description of being in Buddha-nature; as a monad, or as one of the myriad *dharmas*, I am both complete in myself, but also interconnected to everything else around me, in ways that I cannot fathom, nor barely imagine. My self (such as it is), is always already responding "to all that happens in the universe." Within each occurring phenomenon, this is repeated; as something comes to be, it has, immanently, everything else as a possibility. A possibility is always an opening. Something that *may* come to be as a possibility opens me to a different decision in the world. If everything is planned out, if there is no possibility of something different occurring, then nothing can come forward; everything that is must already be. Leibniz, via Stambaugh, allows for worlds to open outwards into other worlds; despite the finitude of this worldlet, I remain infinite in

---

40 Ibid.

the possibilities — as interpenetrations, reflections, and refractions — available through infinite worlds.

Heidegger perhaps echoes the sentiment or understanding of *mu* more clearly than any other modern philosopher when he describes this "open" in *Contributions*; he describes the open "as the unprotectedness of the carrying out of thrownness; both belonging together as the clearing of self-concealing. The 'there' as ap-propriated in the event." The clearing of self-clearing repeats and opens up the possibility of *mu* as a touchstone. The task of understanding the emptiness of emptiness is emptiness requires unprotectedness as practice. Unprotectedness becomes an opportunity to the possibility of the open.

6

Everything is Nothing

In the late Joan Stambaugh's comparative study of three Japanese philosophers — Dōgen, Hisamatsu (whom we will regrettably not write about), and Keiji Nishitani, she begins her thinking of Nishitani with a discussion of his view of the difference between the "I" and what Nishitani calls "the self itself," or the "the self as such." This self — what Stambaugh calls the "true self" — is the originary ground for the "life process." The "I" works as a construct, a something projected forward, as a "frame of interpretation that is added to experience," while the true self is "the *source* of the life process."[1] This self is only understood from *beyond* an ordinary consciousness; it cannot be apprehended by our logical, rational, prosaic selves — it cannot be conceived of within the everyday. This original self, for Nishitani, is *no (particular) thing*; it is an originary and felt ground, one which cannot even be thought but perhaps, with Heidegger, only surrendered into.

While comparing Heidegger's thinking of being with Dōgen's conception of *Buddha-nature* is a dangerous exercise (as already admitted), finding, within Nishitani, echoes of Heidegger's thinking is not so farfetched. Indeed, Nishitani studied with Heidegger in Freiburg from 1937 through 1939 and his teacher Nishida Kitaro was in communication with Heidegger prior

---

1   Joan Stambaugh, *The Formless Self* (Albany: State University of New York Press, 1999), 101.

to that time. The entire Kyoto school, of which Nishitani was a major participant, openly recognized their debt to the original thinking of Heidegger. But this is not to say that they were mere Heideggerians in any sense of the word; indeed, what the Kyoto school managed to do was to offer, perhaps for the first time, an intellectual bridge between two conceptions of being, two thinkings towards the question of somethingness and nothingness. In 1937, when Nishitani began studying with Heidegger, the German was already struggling with issues of nihilism as well as ideas towards the clearing, ideas echoed, as we have already seen, in the works of Dōgen.

For Nishitani, as for Heidegger and Dōgen, how things "are" is of a concern, and, even more so, how things are in relation to how *we are* is even more of a concern. In *Religion and Nothingness,* Nishitani describes the limited way we normally relate to phenomena only from our own "field of consciousness," a consciousness that always perceives from with the "citadel of the self," a kind of aporetic Platonic cave without exit. Nishitani writes that

> to look at things from the standpoint of the self is always to see things as merely as objects, that is, to look at things from without from a field within the self. It means assuming a position vis-à-vis things from which self and things remain fundamentally separated from one another. This standpoint of separation of subject and object, or opposition between within or without, is what we call the field of "consciousness.[2]

So far at least, Nishitani is following a familiar problem; that of how things *present* themselves to us, and to how we r*epresent* them. Nishitani writes that "for all our talk about the reality of things, things do not truly display their *real* reality to us."[3] What Nishitani describes is a dilemma that we are already familiar

---

2   Keiji Nishitani, *Religion and Nothingness,* trans. Jan Van Bragt (Berkeley: University of California Press, 1982), 9.

3   Ibid.

with; the world, on a prosaic, everyday level, resists our entrée into it. What we experience as things are mere *representations* of entities, and, from within the self, we look out to a field of things. We remain constantly separated — not only from other things — but from our very selves. Nishitani presents this existential dilemma in a stark light. He writes:

> The field that lies at the ground of our everyday lives is the field of essential separation between self and things, the field of consciousness, within which a real self-presentation of reality cannot take place at all. Within it, reality appears only in shape of shattered fragments, only in the shape of ineluctable self-contradictions.[4]

Nishitani is well aware of the echoing of basic psychological principles that his ideas draw on, evoking both Descartes and Freud in describing an essential dualism between self and world, and critiquing the conception of a world exemplified by the thinking of the *res cogitans* and *res extensa*. He is also acutely aware of the impositions that such thinking from the within have. The "ineluctable self-contradictions" of modern, ordered, scientific life epitomized in a duality separating subject and object, and thing from world, destroy what is most human, what is most natural, most original in our relationship to the world. Echoing Heidegger's ruthless critique of the overtaking by science of the original impetus of thinking in *The End of Philosophy and the Task of Thinking*,[5] Nishitani writes that this self-contradiction causes man

> to surround himself with a cold lifeless world. Inevitably, each individual ego became like a lonely but well-fortified island floating on a sea of dead matter. The life was snuffed

---

4 Ibid., 10.
5 The original date of publication of *Shūkyō to wa Nanika* is 1961, while *Zur Sache des Denkens* appeared in German in 1969, though it was published first in French in 1966.

out of nature and the things of nature; the living stream that flowed at the bottom of man and all things, and kept them bound together, dried up.[6]

Nishitani seeks to move us beyond that thinking which "dries up," to get beyond the objectification of the thing by a subject, a thinking which leaves us always separate from an authentic and real encounter with the world. As long as we are encased within what Nishitani calls the "person-centered person," we remain, for Nishitani, "well-fortified islands floating on a sea of dead matter." The empirical, scientific thinking which promotes this duality and disallows for an integral, unified conception of the world is not immune to the nihility which both Nishitani and Heidegger claim is the basis of a movement "towards a new beginning." Nishitani writes that "the horizon on which such doubt occurs […] is a horizon opening up to the ground of human existence itself."[7] Like Heidegger, Nishitani sees in the aporia of rational thinking a "way out," a way beyond the nihilism of modern, scientific thinking, a thinking which leads — if unchecked — directly, for both thinkers, to Auschwitz and Hiroshima. Nishitani describes Dostoevsky's evocation of the struggles in *Notes from the Underground* as "a paradoxical position from which the world makes itself present to us," in which we are "unable to affirm, unable to deny, and [have] no recourse left but to bang one's head against it."[8] And yet, it is precisely at the point where the Underground Man bangs his head, at the point when the "awareness of nihility penetrating deep beneath the world of natural laws and human rationality with which science is preoccupied"[9] that an opening occurs. This "awareness of nihility opens up a horizon that enables a freedom beyond necessity and life beyond rationality."[10] Nishitani's focus is on moving through or beyond this limit of nihility, but the process itself is

---

6   Nishitani, *Religion and Nothingness*, 11.
7   Ibid., 46.
8   Ibid., 48.
9   Ibid.
10 Ibid.

one which must be arrived at. It is a universal that all of us, "even the scientist," must eventually face as we experience our limits, the horizon of our finitude.

But the difficulty, faced so often in contemporary thought — whether by Dostoyevsky, Nietzsche, Kierkegaard, and even Heidegger — is that nihilism risks becoming a final limit, a horizon in which the destructive energies of such thinking do not allow one to pass through to the other side, but which root us instead in an unsustainable position of doubt and resignation. The leap which Heidegger proposes, and which Nishitani finds support for in both Western thought (notably in the thinking of Meister Eckhart) as well as in the thinking of his own native Japan, involves a surrender into *ekstasis*. However, Nishitani's understanding of the process of ecstasy is different from Heidegger's; while Heidegger understands *ekstasis* as the process through which Dasein projects itself onto the horizon, a "towards which" the temporal ecstasies reach, Nishitani views ecstasy as the "mode of being wherein the self *is* in itself at the point that it has stepped over itself."[11] The self then is eclipsed or occluded by the presence of the self left behind. Nishitani cautions, however, that this is not enough. Ecstasy is the movement of the self to the opening of the self, to finding the ground of the self; it is through what Nishitani calls negation-*sive*-affirmation where understanding moves from a recognition of nothingness towards an authentic encounter with being as being. In effect, Nishitani is returning our*selves* to ourselves, not as emaciated echoes of real beings — which might be the case in Western nihilism, and which *is* the case for Dostoyevsky's Underground Man — but as complete, fully present individuals.

While nihilism comes to mean the rejection of all things, and becomes, via its rejection, some*thing*, the concept negation-*sive*-affirmation is what Nishitani calls absolute — or true — nothingness. Absolute nothingness, Nishitani is at pains to make clear, is not just something behind a person or a phenomena, nor is it a metaphor. "True nothingness," he writes, "means that there is

---

11   Ibid., 68.

no thing that in nothingness, and this is *absolute nothingness*."[12]
With absolute nothingness, Nishitani is taking us to the edge of
possible comprehension; indeed, he writes that this is a concept
that cannot be conceived as such. He writes, "absolute nothingness, wherein even that 'is' is negated, is not possible as a
nothingness that is thought, but only *as a nothingness that is
lived.*"[13] To experience this requires "an existential conversion,
a change of heart within man himself."[14] And it is through this
conversion, this moving through the self, that one can arrive at
an authentic and real encounter with the self as a self (and not
as a constructed, artificial self).

The concept that Nishitani points us towards — a view of absolute nothingness not as a nihilistic dystopia but rather a nothingness which is both liberatory and soteriological — has a long
history amongst traditional Buddhist thinkers. Dōgen grapples
with it, but even prior to Dōgen, the concept of *śūnyatā,* or absolute nothingness, is a fundamental idea on which Buddhism
itself is grounded, and it remains the fundamental difference in
ontological understanding of world between the East and the
West. In philosophical terms, the concept is perhaps first and
best dealt with by Nāgārjuna in the *Mūlamadhyamaka-kārikā*
from the 2nd century CE. The *Mūlamadhyamaka-kārikā,* or
Fundamental Wisdom of the Middle Way, works through a series of ontological and epistemological contradictions which
amount to arguing that the world, or world, is first empty of
essence, and that no thing or *dharma* has independent being;
that all thoughts, things, emotions and phenomena arise from
a vast flux of interdependent origination, a wellspring of influences which have no original source. This dependent origination, or *pratītyasamutpāda,* points to the essential emptiness of
each "thing" or phenomena. For if no thing has a unique, discrete "self," and is instead a mere gathering point — a *gathering
towards* — of influence, of phenomena, of echoes and traces (to

---

12 Ibid., 70.
13 Ibid.
14 Ibid.

echo Derrida), then each thing is empty of inherent existence. Nāgārjuna writes in the *Mūlamadhyamaka-kārikā* that whatever comes into "being dependent on another," that is, all phenomenological occurrences,

> is not identical to that thing
> Nor is it different from it.
> Therefore it is neither nonexistent in time nor permanent.[15]

While Nāgārjuna is detailing here a brief re-examination of the concept of dependent origination, that is, that it is impossible to separate one phenomena from another, that indeed each thing is intimately connected to each other, a deeper reading reveals that emptiness itself, if dealt with ontologically, must be "neither nonexistent in time nor permanent." If Nāgārjuna had stopped there, we could dismiss him as being a mere materialist, or a nihilist committed to the negative. He goes further, however, and reveals that we can't rest in simply saying that "this is empty," and "that is empty," (to abide in emptiness would be the same as abiding in the essential). Nāgārjuna writes that emptiness must be a concept that is itself treated as empty of essential existence. To treat it otherwise would be to fall into the same trap of metaphysical thinking that has bedeviled and beguiled so many. We can't abide in emptiness, we can't take refuge in the concept as a substitute for fullness, for essence, but we must overthrow the very idea of emptiness as well. To say emptiness "is" is to "grasp for permanence." To say "it is not" is to fall into "the view of nihilism." Nāgārjuna counsels instead that a "wise person does not say "exists" or "does not exist" and simply allows for phenomena, empty of all inherent essence, to simply be, to perdure without counsel. To do otherwise is dangerous; he warns that "by a misperception of emptiness, a person of little intelligence

---

15 Nāgārjuna, *The Fundamental Wisdom of The Middle Way: Nāgārjuna's Mūlamadhyamakakārika,* trans. Jay L. Garfield (New York: Oxford University Press, 1995), 36.

is destroyed like a snake incorrectly seized."[16] Equally, "for him to whom emptiness is clear, everything becomes clear."[17]

Nothingness's Fullness

For Nishitani, the understanding of *śūnyatā* is the central ground from which to view all things, and to stand there is, with Nāgārjuna, to see clearly. While Heidegger seemed to struggle with the concept of transcendence, viewing the leap as at times a leap to "somewhere,"[18] a leap which "jettisons and leaves behind everything conventional,"[19] for Nishitani "such a field cannot lie on a far side, beyond *this* world and *this* earthly life of ours, as something merely transcendent." The leap must be resolutely fixed to "this side," and paraphrasing Eckhart, Nishitani claims the ground for an authentic becoming lies "nearer to the self than the self is to itself." Our question then, is where to locate it?

Śūnyatā for Nishitani is "the point at which we become manifest in our own suchness as concrete human beings,"[20] but it is also, at the same time, the point "at which everything around us becomes manifest in its own suchness." Being as absolute nothingness is, therefore, a locus through which suchness (such as it is) manifests itself, if only temporally, into form in a spatio-temporal context. It is the ground through which something comes to be, but it is a something devoid of independent essence. This standpoint of absolute nothingness serves as a break from a false identification with self-attachment and notions of perpetuity as it denies and distances itself from any sense of the self being shackled or tied to being. Like the grasping of phenomena in

---

16 Ibid., 68.

17 Ibid.

18 Heidegger's views are not this clear. At times, he seems to locate the leap as leading to another place, a transcendent movement, at others, as in the case of das offen the location seems resolutely already here.

19 Martin Heidegger, *Contributions to Philosophy (Of the Event),* trans. Richard Rojcewicz and Daniela Vallega-Neu (Bloomington: Indiana University Press, 2012), 179.

20 Nishitani, *Religion and Nothingness,* 90.

Heidegger, where the object constantly withdraws from itself, so emptiness, whenever confronted, withdraws as well. Each time we turn to face emptiness, it defies objective representation; no sooner have we named it than it withdraws into hiding like an octopus behind a cloud of ink. Emptiness confounds and disassembles any notion of fixity or permanency. Nishitani writes:

> As a valley unfathomably deep may be imagined set within an endless expanse of sky, so it is with nihility and emptiness. But the sky we have in mind here is more than the vault above that spreads out far and wide over the valley below. It is a cosmic sky enveloping the earth and man and the countless legions of stars that move and have their being within it. It lies beneath the ground we tread, its bottom reaching beneath the valleys bottom. If the place where the omnipresent God resides be called heaven, then heaven would also have to reach beneath the bottomless pit of hell: heaven would be an abyss for hell. This is the sense on which emptiness is an abyss for nihility.[21]

Emptiness exceeds any understanding of itself, and while Nishitani readily acknowledges the failure of language in describing *śūnyatā,* the most we can hope for is an oblique description of emptiness's continual withdrawal. *Śūnyatā* as absolute emptiness is contrasted to the ontological conception of nihilism. Nihilism as an idea has, as a belief or understanding of nothingness, a political, and ontological significance as something in the world, *even if that something is nothing. Śūnyatā* is distinguished in the quote above by its empty vastness, the extent of its self which, rather than being nothing, is *no thing;*[22] no thing which, if named, becomes something. *Śūnyatā* must remain withdrawn, and yet is ever present, absolute in its absence.

---

21 Ibid., 98.

22 In Advaita Vedanta, there is an expression — *neti, neti* — which is an analytical meditation used to help a practitioner identify what "is not" Brahma. *Neti, neti* means "not that, not that" and the practice corresponds to *the via Negativa* tradition in the West.

Śūnyatā is the abyss through which nihility comes to be, it is the ground for nothingness.

Nihility as a concept alienates and divides one from the other, object from subject, name from phenomenon, man from woman; it is the abyss across which almost nothing can pass, and we abide separate from each other, from things, from world, rather than in community. For Nishitani, people give names to persons and things, in part to bridge the unbridgeable abyss, and by naming, "suppose that if they know the names, they know that which the names refer to."[23] By naming world, we claim world, we claim ourselves. But this naming is premised in falsehood and inauthenticity, and while the ambiguous becomes certain through language, through rational thinking, the reality of nihility, the reality which says "the flower in my garden is an unknown entity,"[24] becomes instead covered over by an everyday world "which is in its proper element when it traffics in names."[25] The horror of contemporary nihilism is dissolved by an opiate of language.

Nishitani, however, cautions us that though *śūnyatā* encompasses nihilism, it is not in fact the "desolate and bottomless abyss [which] distances even the most intimate of persons or things from each other."[26] *Śūnyatā* as absolute emptiness "points directly to a most intimate encounter with everything that exists."[27] There is, as in Dōgen and even in Heidegger, a sense of soteriological liberation within an honest encounter with emptiness, within an authentic grasping — a perceptive seeing — of *śūnyatā*. To Nishitani, this encounter "takes place at the source of existence common to one and the other and yet at a point where each is truly itself."[28] The field of emptiness becomes the evental site for a self-appropriation by a thing to itself. It is only through a direct experience, a direct, lived insight, into the emp-

23 Nishitani, *Religion and Nothingness*, 100.
24 Ibid., 101.
25 Ibid.
26 Ibid., 102.
27 Ibid.
28 Ibid.

tiness of everything (explicitly not, however, into the *meaninglessness* of everything) that we are free to become that which we authentically are. Through the grasping of the essential nature of true emptiness, we become who we are, not who we have crafted and formed ourselves to be.

With an understanding of Nishitani, it is perhaps time to return to a passage of Dōgen's that we've already considered. He writes in the *Shōbōgenzō* that

> to learn the Buddha way is to learn one's self. To learn one's self is to forget one's self. To forget one's self is to be confirmed by all things. To be confirmed by all things is to effect the dropping off of one's body-and-mind and the mind-and-body of others as well.[29]

Examining the etymological roots of "Buddha-way" first in Sanskrit (*bodhati*) where it means "to awake, know, perceive," and secondly in Pali (*budh*), where it means, "observes, understands," respectively, we can read the above passage as a description of the process through which one realizes, or awakens, to the field of absolute emptiness, to *śūnyatā*. When we awaken to the authentic nature — whether through sudden realization as in the Rinzai tradition of Zen, or through subtle practice as in Dōgen's Soto, or even through the deep, abiding perception and thinking of the essential nature of things as Heidegger would have us do — of the self, we learn the self. But this awakening involves intimately grasping that the self is not the self; and in doing that, we come to forget the self. By forgetting the self, we understand that the self, such as it has been formulated, is empty of inherent existence, that is, it is a mere formation of other forces, a collecting of phenomenological events which serve to, temporarily, come together to form the self. This realization — prosaic if we resist it, yet devastatingly transformative if we allow ourselves to "awaken" to it — is the "dropping off of

---

29 Eihei Dōgen, *The Heart of Dōgen's Shōbōgenzō*, trans. Norman Waddell and Masao Abe (Albany: State University of New York Press, 2002).

one's body-and-mind and the mind-and-body of others as well." If we are seriously to interact with *śūnyatā,* then we must understand that within absolute emptiness, there can be no *thing* as we understand a thing to be. Without thing, there can be no perdurance, without perdurance, no time. Without time, there can be no transformation. In an instant, we can do away with Heraclitus's river; for without a thing to change, how can some thing change? How can no thing (what was not there) become some thing (a thing that is there)?

Nishitani describes this stance, via Dōgen, as the "knowing of non-knowing." It is, as played on the field of emptiness, a position of authenticity in which, to borrow from Heidegger, one's own appropriation takes place; it is then the evental exposure of the self to the self, without interference. Nishitani writes:

> It is the point at which the self is truly on its own home-ground. Here plants and trees have penetrated to the bottom to be themselves; here tiles and stones are through and through tiles and stones; and here, too, in self-identity with everything, the self is radically itself. This is the knowing of non-knowing, the field of emptiness itself.[30]

Nishitani describes a dropping-down into the field of absolute emptiness, a distancing of the rational from world itself, which, in *śūnyatā,* opens one up to the possibility of something other, something which radically already exists, but is empty of inherent existence; that is world as an un-reified concept. Nishitani describes the authentic experience not only of the self *coming to the self,* but of all things — not only tiles and stones and plants and trees but also desks and coffee cups — universes and plastic bags even — coming to their original selves, which of course is not a "self" at all, but rather the event of *śūnyatā.* Heidegger seems to lead us in this direction as well when he writes in *Contributions* that inceptual thinking (as meditation) is "the carrying out and preparing for the resonating and the interplay, first

---

30 Nishitani, *Religion and Nothingness,* 110.

of all as a transition [*Übergang*] and as such is a down-going [*Unter-gang*]."[31] While neither description can satisfy the analytic, both point us towards a new understanding of world; a world that is not formed by materialist, discrete, atomistic entities, not simply from Platonic ideas which resist apprehension. Rather, both direct us to an understanding of world which is radical in its uncertainty, which resonates in inter-penetration of phenomena, and which points to an experience of nihility as a mere passing-through, a moving past, and which prepares us for, with Heidegger, a "new beginning," and, with Nishitani, the field of emptiness, or *śūnyatā*.

Nishitani conceives of this field as "a field that goes beyond consciousness and intellect."[32] Therefore, beyond language, and even a conception of nothingness; this is the ground on which the "knowing of non-knowing" can take place. It must be a ground where *thing* as an un-grasped, un-taken, un-seized concept is able to come into being (whatever that looks like), a ground where a *thing* is allowed to be, *as it is.* This is different from mere, everyday nihility. Nihilism, for Nishitani, is constrained by always "being viewed from the side of existence." That is, we are limited in viewing nothingness always from the perception of being, from something, and as such, nihility is always seen in "opposition to being, *a relative nothingness.*"[33] Nihilism is the experience of nothingness from the experience of essence, and as such is always negatively contrasted to it. Nihility can never be authentic because by stating that something is nothingness, it denies the something which describes it; it remains, therefore, a logical impossibility. For Nishitani, absolute nothingness, or *śūnyatā,* is emptied even of the representation of emptiness; there is no thing that is not already always empty of inherent existence, *including the concept of nothingness itself.* In Nishitani, this root emptiness — universal and infinite, resistant to any formulation — is key; *śūnyatā* binds nothingness's

---

31 Heidegger, *Contributions to Philosophy (Of the Event),* 53.

32 Nishitani, *Religion and Nothingness,* 121.

33 Ibid., 123.

vacuum with beingness's exhaustiveness. For Nishitani, absolute emptiness is resolutely not the affirmation of nothingness; rather, "the field of emptiness stands opened at the very point that things emerge into being."[34] And it is this emergency of being that restores to being its *essential being* which nihility denied it. This is not to say that we have done away with absolute nothingness; in fact, we have embraced it all the more fully, giving the field of *śūnyatā* an ontological presence, if only as the birthplace of authentic being. On the field of *śūnyatā*,

> each and everything that is recovers once again its power of concentration by gathering itself into itself. All are returned to the possibility of existence. Each thing is restored anew to its own virtues — that individual capacity that each thing possesses as display of its own possibility of existence.[35]

Nishitani describes a return of a thing to itself through the clarifying and transformative process of arriving at an authentic experience of its own *possibilities*. He writes that

> emptiness might be called the field of "be-ification" (*Ichtung*) in contrast to nihility which is the field of "nullification" (*Nichtung*). To speak in Nietzschean terms, this field of be-ification is the field of the Great Affirmation, where we can say Yes to all things.[36]

In this way, he returns being to being through the exposure of being to its own nullity, to its own inherent substancelessness, and by so doing, gives back to being substance (though transformed), gives back what Nishitani calls *selfness*. The thing, reunited with its self-nature, after passage through the field of absolute emptiness, is, at first glance the same as it was before; the cup, the person, the forest, all seem to be the same, but ac-

---

34 Ibid.
35 Ibid.
36 Ibid., 124.

cording to Nishitani, a fundamental change has occurred. Prior to its transformation, when it was still viewed as either *merely* an object in the material world, or as a representation of an *eidos* or experience of the *noumena,* a thing was viewed solely in terms of it being there for one, or as an object in space; after traversing the field of absolute nothingness, a thing is expressed no longer as a single, discrete phenomenon, nor even as a rendering of something else (as in Plato and Kant); rather, it "is disclosed precisely as something that cannot be so expressed."[37] Selfness cannot be expressed within quotidian reason; it exceeds language, and it is only through an authentic experience of absolute nothing that something (be it a person or a cup) attains its understanding — its self-being — fully.

On the field of *śūnyatā,* a thing emerges as itself, and beyond such categories as substance, quality, quantity; it emerges in absolute nothingness and becomes "master of itself."[38] In this sense it is as a mode of being which Nishitani calls "autonomous," but not in the sense that a thing is free to choose which "face" to show us. Rather, it is a

> mode of being that has nothing to do with our representations or judgements; yet it is not on the back side, or hidden aspect of things. Such expressions already imply a view of things from where *we* stand. On its own home-ground, a thing has no front and no back. It is purely and simply itself, as it is in its selfness and nothing more.[39]

With the recognition of *śūnyatā* as the "home-ground," which, with Heidegger we can see as the Abgrund, as that ground below the ground, as the primordial, the abyssal ground, the thing becomes — is allowed to be — itself, and is neither substance nor subject; *it is in its selfness and nothing more.* If we are, with Nishitani, to imagine this "nothing more," it must resist language, and

37 Ibid., 124.
38 Ibid., 127.
39 Ibid.

even perhaps imagination. Nishitani turns to the poet Bashō to clarify the concept. Bashō writes:

> From the pine tree
> learn of the pine tree,
> And from the bamboo
> of the bamboo.

Nishitani explains that if we are to practice an authentic learning, or thinking, about the pine tree, we must place ourselves in the mode of being of the pine tree. If we attempt instead to codify and name the bamboo (*Acidosasa chinensis*), placing it in the context of something else, or in relation to another, we imprison it within a context of scientific knowledge which denies, or at least elides, the bamboo as it is in that moment, as it is now. Nishitani writes that what Bashō describes is a form of "becoming" the pine tree and the bamboo, of "taking after" the bamboo to stand in its mode of being.

> The mode of being of things in their selfness consists of the fact that things take up a position grounded in themselves and settle themselves on that position. They center in on themselves and do not get scattered.[40]

When the bamboo is denied its selfness, and represented (and thus known and understood) as *Acidosasa chinensis,* it is represented from the standpoint of something external. Even when I make a reference to "bamboo" (or "sunset," "leaf," "lover," "moon" or indeed any *thing*) I am making reference to something external, and from a position of perpetual exteriority, and thereby deny or ignore something essential. In contrast, "bamboo," resting in its own essential selfness, unmediated by my demands upon it, frees the bamboo from being there *for me.* The bamboo, on the field of absolute nothingness, becomes its own inherency, without reference to an other.

---

40 Ibid., 128.

With Nishitani's contemporary description of *śūnyatā*, we can return again to Dōgen's conception of absolute emptiness and understand it more deeply. Dōgen writes:

> Hence every piece of *mu* [*Buddha-nature*] is a touchstone to articulate emptiness; emptiness is the capacity to articulate *mu*. This is not the emptiness of "form is emptiness." "Form is emptiness" does not mean form is forced into emptiness, nor is it making form out of emptiness. It has to be the emptiness of "emptiness is emptiness." The emptiness of "emptiness of emptiness" is a piece of rock in emptiness.[41]

The Buddha-nature (*mu*) of a thing (that is, *all things as all things* have Buddha-nature) encompasses all facets of an apparent phenomenon, revealing the abyssal ground from which it emerges as much as its quantifiable surface, and, as such, form is a pointer (*at that which withdraws*) and is used to "articulate" emptiness, to make manifest that which resolutely remains withdrawn, intangible. We find ourselves again at the very edges of language, attempting to use words to describe some thing that is not (a) thing, and we make it, again, some thing. Our every attempt at a descriptive destroys the concept. Dōgen does not conceive of the destruction of form; form is not merely empty, it is always abyssally empty, bottomless and both existent and non-existent at the same time, present and withdrawn. The field of *śūnyatā* as endlessly withdrawn ground finally allows a thing to perdure in its own selfness, becoming emptiness as emptiness of emptiness.

The Unframing of Nature

In Heidegger's lecture from 1951, "Bauen Wohnen Denken" (and published as a book in 1954, though not translated into English until 1971) Heidegger takes up what we have already seen in Dōgen, Bashō, and Nishitani; to authentically allow something

---

41 Dōgen, *The Heart of Dōgen's Shōbōgenzō,* 72.

to be, and to authentically come into presence with a thing in an original encountering, we must first recognize it as an object there for itself, and *not* there for something or someone else. An object, coming to be on the field of absolute emptiness becomes open to its ownmost possibilities; it dwells in those possibilities. As Bashō counseled in the haiku mentioned above, that "from the pine tree," we should "learn of the pine tree," so Heidegger writes that to exist as a human being, "means to be on the earth as a mortal." For Heidegger *being* on the earth is "to dwell." To dwell means not only to exist, and to inhabit, but to, at the same time, "cherish, and protect, to preserve and care for."[42] Dwelling for Heidegger is not a passive act assumed by someone who lives in a place; to dwell means to be engaged with what it means to exist, what it means to perdure, if only for an instant. Through a series of etymological groundings, Heidegger describes dwelling first as a building or constructing, and of a residing, but more importantly, as the very foundation of who and what we are, *when we are*. Heidegger writes that "the way in which you are and I am, the manner in which we humans *are* on the earth is *Baun,* dwelling."[43] We exist by being, and our being is caught up with a residing in, *a being in,* the world as mortals. We have seen Heidegger's concept of being, or *Sein,* evolve from *Dasein* to *Mitsein,* from being-there to being-with; in dwelling, we find *Sein* engaged in a being-in, or *Insein*. In this way, we are distinct; as Heidegger observed early in his career, as human beings we are always already thrown into a world of mortality; it is our very observation of this that gives to us a sense of wonder, a sense of beingness. To exist in this space of finitude, to inhabit world as a finite object — brilliantly aware and attuned — is to dwell, undisturbed, within the ground of becoming.

As Bashō counsels a quiescent observation of the pine tree, allowing the pine tree to presence *as a pine tree* and *not as my expectation* of a pine tree, so Heidegger demands, for a being to live authentically, that one should allow things to be what they

---

42 Heidegger, *Basic Writings,* 349.

43 Ibid.

are, not what we require them to be; to let the world come to be as the world *be*-comes, and not to, as he writes in "Bauen Wohnen Denken," *turn day into harassed unrest.* To dwell is to be, perhaps, upon the field of *śūnyatā*; it is to exist within the field of absolute emptiness, undeclared, un-reified, unmade for someone, or something, other. It is to exist as the pine tree does, not in relation to, or for someone else; it is simply, purely, to be. There is an ethics at play — environmental or otherwise — here that is often overlooked in scholarship (indeed, to speak of Heidegger and ethics is too quickly to be received with a deep skepticism.) If I "allow" something to be — whether a pine tree, bamboo or even a person — and do not insist it to be something else, to be what I desire it to be, I let that something exist freely. I take up that thing's very being and, by not interfering with it — by not insisting my position in relation to it — I "allow"[44] it to be. I grant it freedom, as it in turn grants me freedom. This is similar to what Nishitani would have us do on the field of *śūnyatā*; in absolute emptiness, a thing exists for itself only, emptied of inherent essence and projected requirements, and able to dwell, or to perdure, in its own essential freedom. In a similar fashion, Dōgen writes, in the "Busshō" fascicle, "the meaning of Buddhanature is absolutely empty, clear and distinct."[45]

Heidegger takes up this idea of freedom in "Bauen Wohnen Denken," linking the German word *bauen,* which means, in a contemporary reading of the word, "to build." Heidegger links *bauen* to its high German origin, which Heidegger reads as "to dwell." He then, in turn, reads this understanding with the Gothic *wunian,* which means "to be at, or to be brought to peace." Returning once again to contemporary German, Heidegger writes that peace, *Friede,* means the free, *das Frye,* and that *das Frye* actually means: *preserved from harm and danger, preserved from something.* To be preserved from something means to be safeguarded, to be, in Heidegger's terminology, therefore *spared.*

---

44 The language of permission, or allowing something to be is problematic here, yet that is exactly what is demanded of us in this case.

45 Dōgen, *The Heart of Dōgen's Shōbōgenzō,* 81.

> To free really means to spare. The sparing itself consists not only in the fact that we do not harm the one whom we spare. Real sparing is something *positive* and takes place when we leave something beforehand in its own nature, when we return it specifically to its being, when we "free" it in the real sense of the word into a preserve of peace. To dwell, to be set at peace, means to remain at peace within the free, the preserve, the free sphere that safeguards each thing in its nature.[46]

Accordingly then, to dwell means to be free, and to be free means to spare, or to be spared. Again, there is an interesting ethics at work here, between the one sparing and the spared; by being free, I am free to spare an other; this is different from the enslaved person who is freed by his master, who is *granted* freedom (a boon which, by the very nature of the master–servant relationship, can always be rescinded). Heidegger does not write that to be free means to be spared; rather to be free *is to spare,* it is to engage in "granting" permission, but in a very rare sense. In sparing we allow something to be preserved, but preserved by *itself*; we open the space for something to self-preserve. This is the active sense in which one spares an other (even an other pine tree). If I spare the pine tree my understanding of it, my *claiming it* (whether this claiming is instrumental through science or technology, or through the simple act of naming doesn't matter; the result remains the same), I allow it to be, within its own time, in its own space. By refusing the claim, I allow it to come forward; I beckon it, and it *be*-comes. Not *through* my invitation, but *alongside* my invitation.

To dwell, then, is also to give, to offer over the space or clearing to allow something to come to be. Heidegger writes that that to dwell is to receive as well as to give.

---

46 Martin Heidegger, *Poetry, Language, Thought,* trans. Albert Hofstadter (New York: Harper & Row, 1971). 149.

Mortals dwell in that they receive the sky as the sky. They leave to the sun and the moon their journey, to the stars their courses, to the seasons their blessing and their inclemency; they do not turn night into day nor day into harassed unrest.[47]

For Heidegger, "allowing" something to be is to receive it, is to enter into a relation with it that is free, and based on care and attentiveness, while at the same time not overwhelming it.

Heidegger writes that "the fundamental character of dwelling is this sparing and preserving."[48] There is a sense of profound hospitality at play in the giving to something the space to presence itself authentically, to present itself within its own field. Heidegger writes that "to save really means to set something free into its own presencing."[49] Dwell, then, comes to mean to allow for being to presence itself in its ownmost, authentic way; the pine tree comes to be when we offer it the space to be; until then, it is a dull representation of what I think a pine tree should be. However, it is only a dull representation for me; my experience of truth is hampered, but not the pine tree's experience. This is perhaps what Heidegger meant when he wrote that "world worlds;" things come to be all the time, but it is only when we can clear our own dross, our own inauthentic experience of world, that we can experience it in its own utmost authenticity.

The way something comes into presence, the way world worlds, is, for Heidegger, through the "gathering" of "the four-fold" (*das Geviert*). A space or location comes to be in the presencing of a thing. The concept is difficult to comprehend, yet deserves our attention. *Das Geviert* is an all too often under-examined idea in Heidegger, and until recently, very little scholarship had been done on it; for the most part, the fourfold has been treated with suspicion and even derision by scholars. In more recent times, however, several philosophers, most notably

---

47 Ibid., 150.
48 Ibid., 149.
49 Ibid., 150.

Graham Harman among them, have begun to take seriously the challenge of the fourfold. For our own purposes, in our reading of Dōgen and in an attempt to open up an *allée* between the two thinkers, the fourfold is a crucial bridge to enjoin the two philosophers.

For Heidegger, a thing comes to be within the fourfold "gathering" of earth, sky, divinities and mortals. To separate one from each is impossible, and to treat one as its own entity is also a mistake; rather, what Heidegger proposes is that for the "simple oneness" of being to take place, it must take place at a confluence in the flow of *das Geviert*. Heidegger describes earth as "the serving bearer, blossoming and fruiting...rising up into plant and animal" while the sky,

> is the vaulting path of the sun, the course of the changing moon, the wandering glitter of the stars, the year's season and their changes, the light and dusk of day, the gloom and glow of night, the clemency and inclemency of the weather, the drifting clouds and blue depth of the ether.[50]

The earth and sky are not discrete, however; each is "already thinking of the other three along with it." It is impossible to separate earth from sky. Equally impossible would be to remove from the "simple oneness" the divinities and mortals. Like the first two, these second two are, though commonly in contrast, in fact, intimates, in that one cannot be without the other three. The gods are "the beckoning messengers of the godhead" while human beings are mortals, but mortal only in that "to die means to be capable of death as death." Like earth and sky, the gods are not contrasted to mortals; rather each comes together, each gathers in the swirling lacunal absence of becoming, and it is through this gathering that the event of a thing occurs, that being *be-comes* and comes to fill the space.

Heidegger uses the description of a bridge to describe how each gathers to the other. A bridge *bridging* quite literally brings

---

50 Ibid., 149.

together two opposing banks; it brings one to the other, but at the same time it also acts as something which denotes a separation. Heidegger writes that one side sets off the other, and in this setting off, the bridge brings the stream into becoming. Though the fourfold may seem a great distance from the Heidegger of the 1920s,[51] we can hear in Heidegger's tool analysis something of the same. The analogy of the broken hammer from *Being and Time* calls to mind a similar dilemma; it is through its very brokenness that we become aware of the hammer, *in its absence*. With the bridge as a gathering, Heidegger writes:

> It brings stream and bank and land into each other's neighborhood. The bridge *gathers* the earth as landscape around the stream. Thus it guides and attends the stream through the meadows. Resting upright in the stream's bed, the bridge-piers bear the swing of the arches that leave the streams to run their course.[52]

The bridge brings into being the stream as it does the banks. Though the bridge is constructed, its gathered self is gathered within a specific location, and brings into being everything else; earth, sky, gods and mortals interconnect and *be*-come through the bridge, with the bridge; the bridge connects, and inter-forms, co-cooperates with other *be*-comings. Heidegger writes that the bridge "*gathers* to itself in *its own way* earth and sky, divinities and mortals."[53] This gathering brings into being the thingness of the bridge; without gathering earth, sky, gods and mortals, nothing is. It is only via gathering that lacunae are filled, if ever so briefly before being regathered. "*As this thing it gathers the fourfold*." Through an inter-*be*-coming the bridge *be*-comes because it gathers, yet the gathering itself brings the bridge to

---

51 According to Andrew J. Mitchell's *The Fourfold: Reading the Late Heidegger* (Evanston: Northwestern Press University, 2015), Heidegger first uses the concept of the fourfold (*das Geivert*) in the *Bremen Lectures* of 1949.

52 Heidegger, *Poetry, Language, Thought,* 152.

53 Ibid., 153.

a *be*-coming; the two are inter-articulated events which both, through allowing for the one, allows for the other.

Through the gathering of the fourfold, a lacunate absence is filled with the thing, and this thing, through the gathering, takes place, *as an evental becoming of itself.* The relationship between the thing becoming and the event's location is intricate; neither presages the other, nor is one in an hierarchical relation with the other.

> [T]he bridge does not first come to a location to stand in it; rather, a location comes into existence only by virtue of the bridge. The bridge is a thing; it gathers the fourfold, but in such a way that it allows for a site for the fourfold.[54]

Allowing a site for the fourfold creates space; location brings space into being, it opens up space, if only by defining it negatively. Space becomes in the wake of a thing's imposition upon it. Heidegger writes that the bridge, "as such a thing [...] allows a space into which earth and heaven, divinities and mortals are admitted."[55] These spaces become intervals, pauses in *be-coming* which allow, if only for a moment, for an phenomena intervening in space to become itself.

Man dwells amidst space, we exist amongst things, and we exist, as things, between things in spaces that open up between locatable and emerging points. Between the points exists an un-locatable other, something which is not me, nor you, nor desk, or lecture hall; rather it is un-gathered space, space which has yet to come.[56] And yet, for Heidegger, to say that mortals are, "is to say that in dwelling they persist through spaces by virtue of their stay among things and locations." We exist as locatable gatherings which pervade and persist for limited becomings, reordered and always already becoming something else, tem-

---

54 Ibid., 154.

55 Ibid., 155.

56 The original term for the Buddha in Sanskrit was *Tathagata*, or "the one thus gone," yet *Tathagata* can also mean "the one not yet come." We can perhaps think of the ungathered space as that which has not yet come.

porally persistent, if only temporarily. As a result, we are never completely here, never merely here. I exist over there in a future direction as I exist still in a remembered past in the doorway I just passed through, in the eyes of a forgotten friend, or in the well I fell into as a child. *I am never merely here.*

In "Uji," we encounter Dōgen exploring a similar idea. For Dōgen, it is clear that the self is never merely here; rather the self, is, as with all things, always already empty of inherent existence. And yet, as we have seen, this view of the self as empty is not the same as a nihilistic, dystopian outlook. For Dōgen, the self, as with all things, exists everywhere, as all things. Yet this is not mere holism; holism restricts us to imagining that there is no definite thing in the world — holism and nihilism are intricately linked, and, at least for Buddhism and Heidegger, neither can sustain itself. Rather, for Dōgen, "we set the self out in array and make that the whole world."[57] By recognizing our entire extension as an infinite one, we thereby rid ourselves of the atomistic, determined locator of traditional ontology. *I am never merely here.* Dōgen, using time (*uji*) as being, writes:

> We must see all the various things of the whole world as so many times. These things do not get in each other's way any more than various times get in each other's way. [...] We set our self out in array, and we see that.[58]

Viewing the self not as merely a discrete, single entity, yet also refusing the view that sees the self as an amorphous extension of all matter, both Heidegger (at least here) and Dōgen (as well as the entire Buddhist canon, to a greater or lesser degree) view the self as both existent and non-existent, divisible and indivisible, as something and nothing; phenomena perdures, empty however of inherent existence, yet overflowing with extrinsic *eventings* (each of which is equally empty of inherency.) This gives the effect of extensible solidity, of permanency, yet is as much in the

---

57 Dōgen, *The Heart of Dōgen's Shōbōgenzō,* 49.
58 Ibid.

flux and flow of *be*-coming as Heraclitus's river. Similarly, in the story of Indra's Net, in which all things are infinitely connected yet also actively enunciated as discrete, interstitial confluences of waypoints and gatherings, distinct and separate, finite in their being, yet infinitely perduring, makes more sense to our understanding of what is happening; a thing exists as a distinct, coming together, a gathering, and yet that existence, rather than being infinite, is in a constant process of change, of *re*-dispersal and *re*-gathering. Being here becomes not a fixed point, analyzable and able to be identified and named; rather, being is always a becoming, always a becoming something else.

This thinking of gatherings and dispersals should point us towards another concept of Heidegger's, that of enframing, or *Gestell*. While used in concert with his questioning of technology, the term itself, as a gathering, can help us in understanding Dōgen. For Heidegger, the process of enframing as a gathering is a process of, amongst others, "producing and presenting," in which "what presences [can] come forth into unconcealment."[59] This is deeply tied to the process of *alētheia,* in which that which has been forgotten, or covered up, is re-appropriated, made to come forward. Heidegger writes:

> Enframing is the gathering together which belongs to that setting-upon which challenges man and puts him in position to reveal the actual, in the mode of ordering, as standing reserve. As the one who is challenged forth in this way, man stands within the essential realm of enframing.[60]

We are never free from the process of gathering and enframing — we stand within it — but it is in our disposition that allows for an authentic recognition of this realm. *Lethe* covers and disperses authentic becoming, but is through the exposure — the leap — that the event of gathering as truth takes place. While

---

59   Martin Heidegger, *Basic Writings,* ed. David Farrell Krell (New York: Harper & Row, 1977). 326.

60   Ibid., 329.

this gathering unfolds primordially in the gathering of the mountain chain, it is in the ordered challenging that what actually is can be experienced.

Like Dōgen, who counsels that "you must not by your own maneuvering make it into nothingness; you must not force it into being," so Heidegger cautions that the "destining of revealing" is "never a fate that compels."[61] The free, uncompelled unconcealment of that which is, is the essence of freedom. A thing must become revealed not through will, but through allowing of it to come forth. Heidegger writes:

> Freedom is that which conceals in a way that opens to light, in whose clearing shimmers the veil that hides the essential occurrence of all truth and lets the veil appear as what veils. Freedom is the realm of the destining that at any given time starts a revealing on its way.[62]

Through the gathering of the enframing, we avail ourselves to the opening of a being's *be*-coming. The destining is our practice of becoming. Through this,

> man becomes truly free only insofar as he belongs to the realm of destining and so becomes one who listens, though not one who obeys.[63]

In the following chapter, we will take up what the being who listens, as the being who practices, looks like.

---

61 Ibid., 330.
62 Ibid.
63 Ibid.

7

The Practice of Thinking

We ended the previous chapter with a discussion of Heidegger's enigmatic thinking of the enframing, and with a call towards the freedom that be-comes the one who listens, and its opposing "unfreedom" to the one who merely obeys. It must be noted that it is rather easy to profess an understanding of nothingness and emptiness as a scholastic exercise, as a writing on a subject, but it is far harder to internalize the thoughts of Heidegger and Dōgen, to truly take up, as a practice, *and as an ethics,* what they have proposed. For neither thinker would accept mere book learning, mere cogitation on a subject already known, as authentic understanding. The thinking that they call us to take up is transformative, and in that sense, according to at least these two, it is then vital. Contemporary philosophy, as it is studied in most universities (and unfortunately this the only place it is too often studied) is far removed both from the exertions of Dōgen (and of many religious practicioners), as well as the thinking about thinking taken up, and practiced, by Heidegger. Indeed, Schopenhauer, quoted in an essay by Pierre Hadot entitled "Philosophy as a Way of Life," described this type of scholastic exercise as "mere fencing in front of a mirror."[1] In the essay, Hadot draws out the movement of philosophy from a "practice" of

---

1   Pierre Hadot, *Philosophy as a Way of Life,* trans. Michael Chase (Oxford: Blackwell Publishing, 1995), 270.

antiquity in which philosophy "was a mode of existing-in-the-world, which had to be practiced at each instant," towards its inevitable co-option by Christianity and the intellectual scholastic tradition in which philosophy becomes a "purely theoretical and abstract activity."[2] This trend continues and is seen today in the modern university, where, instead of a practice, philosophy becomes a discourse and one in which education is "no longer directed towards people who [are] to be educated with a view to becoming fully developed human beings, but to specialists, in order that they might learn how to train other specialists."[3] This results in a discursive "construction of a technical jargon reserved for specialists,"[4] which, for Hadot as for Heidegger and Dōgen, is a far cry from the vital nature that thinking calls us towards. In opposition to this stultification, Hadot writes that in ancient philosophy, "[thinking] is a conversion, a transformation of one's way of being and living, and a quest for wisdom."[5] Philosophy then, to Hadot, is a critical practice of thinking which takes up thought as a craft to be handled with the express purpose of deepening the human experience. Philosophy is, for Hadot, overly enmeshed in technical jargon which permanently deracinates and impoverishes thinking. In the same quote by Schopenhauer listed above, Hadot closes by writing "And yet, if there is one thing desirable in the world, it is to see a ray of light fall onto the darkness of our lives, shedding some kind of light on the mysterious enigma of our lives."[6]

In this chapter, we hope to begin to unpack what it means to listen, or rather, what it means to avail oneself to the opening of the event of truth, whether this is a thinking of *alētheia,* a "standing-in" in the abyssal between, or a practice of remaining within *śūnyatā* of radical emptiness. This thinking demands a practice towards thinking, which in turn is a thinking towards practice, a practice which is the only way of approaching, or

---

2   Ibid., 265.

3   Ibid., 270.

4   Ibid., 272.

5   Ibid., 275.

6   Ibid., 271.

thinking, with Heidegger, the new beginning. What Heidegger proposes in *Contributions* is not possible from the comfort of a desk, or from the lectern of a classroom; it is a thinking towards a new beginning, an inceptual leap into an abyssal between, and as such can only be taken up *by the rare*. As long as these words are kept safely within a text, as long as they are safely isolated as mere theory, they can never have the revolutionary import that Heidegger seems to demand. We take action towards the practice of thinking, by invoking the world to find ourselves with/in the world. This can never happen within the desiccated leaves of books, in words set in ink long ago dried; it must be a practice taken up and taken into the world.[7]

A similar requirement is made by Dōgen, and in a sense this is easier to practice. Buddhism is, after all, on one level a religion,[8] and as such there are clear rules for practice already laid down. We avoid the pitfalls and risks in Buddhism that exist in philosophy, in that there is a soteriological authority already knit into the fabric of Buddhist philosophy. That said, however, perhaps precisely what gives Buddhism its soteriology is the form of practice. Simply reading about Buddhism will never result in anything beyond Schopenhaurian "fencing." Buddhism, in whatever sect, must be taken up in order to be "understood." Indeed, the Buddha's last words are said to have been "achieve completion through *appamāda*."[9] *Appamāda* in Pali (the original language of the Buddha, and in which his original teachings were transcribed) refers to heedfulness, or diligence, or even conscientiousness; while none of these words directly refer to

---

7   Of course, we must also be cautious here, considering Heidegger's past with the political philosophy of National Socialism. It is impossible to ignore that one key aspect of this philosophy was taking action in the world, and so, with the history of the Holocaust (and of the Japanese imperial occupations), we must engage with these thinkers with a delicate caution, ever mindful of the horrendous pitfalls that lie in wait.

8   Though at its core Buddhism is a philosophy, and perhaps even the first psychology, the rules and rituals surrounding it anchor it firmly as a religion.

9   Thanissaro Bhikkhu, "The Practice in a Word," *Access to Insight* (bcbs Edition), 5 June 2010, http://www.accesstoinsight.org/lib/authors/thanissaro/inaword.html.

practice as such, they seem to point us towards an implementation of ethical principles which, when undertaken, result in a deeper, more profound experience of life.

Simply Sitting

An imprecation towards transformative change must emerge in any authentic reading of Dōgen, if we take what he says seriously; with Dōgen, theory is never a substitute for the fundamental practice of *zazen* or "just sitting." For Dōgen, the awareness of the dharma, of the emptiness of all things, is based first in *physical* practice, the practice of *sitting,* a practice we should go towards "as unhesitatingly as you would brush a fire from the top of your head.[10]" In sitting, we begin to attune our mind towards, ultimately, absolute emptiness.

In the "Zazengi" fascicle of the *Shōbōgenzō,* or "The Principles of Zazen," a document as close to an instruction manual as we can find in philosophy, Dōgen instructs that, in addition to finding a "quiet place" and "not allowing drafts of air, mist, rain, or dew to enter," we must cast aside "involvements of any kind." With Dōgen, it is clear; there is nothing in the kōans, nothing in the philosophy to replace the simple practice of *zazen,* or "just sitting." Sitting is a preparation *towards,* a strengthening and quieting which will allow one to enter the realm of "just seeing," or true perception, of *śūnyatā.* In explicit directions, he tells us to sit in the quiet space, upright, "in correct bodily posture." We are told not to lean to the left or the right, and neither forward nor backward. These are the basic instructions, and do not involve mind at all. In full or half lotus, we exhale deeply and begin. Dōgen advises that "[z]azen is not thinking good; it is not thinking bad. It is not mental activity of any kind; it is not contemplation or reflection. [...] you must cast off your sitting [so that nothing remains]."[11] *Zazen* is about availing yourself to

---

10 Eihei Dōgen, *The Heart of Dōgen's Shōbōgenzō,* trans. Norman Waddell and Masao Abe (Albany: State University of New York Press, 2002), 110.

11 Ibid.

the ground of absolute stillness, of coming to *that* clearing in which what is manifest may manifest itself, may come forward. Dōgen cautions that *zazen* is not about thinking; instead he proposes a movement that, through practice, goes beyond thinking. He writes that "as you sit, meditating silently and immovably, think of not thinking. What is thinking of not thinking? Nonthinking. This, in and of itself, is the art of *zazen*."[12] "Not thinking" is merely a negation of thought, an intellectual exercise that may be practiced by anyone; it is simply a nihilistic rejection of thought; "nonthinking" evokes that which is not perceived by mind, by our senses, that which is not, but is. For Dōgen, *zazen* is not just meditation; by engaging in nonthinking within the field of absolute nothingness, we pass through the "gate of great repose and bliss." The understanding of body-and-mind-falling off, of self becoming non-self is the attainment of "undefiled practice-realization."[13]

Words Fail Us

Though less explicit directions are given by Heidegger, a sense of the central role practice plays in both thinking and *be*-coming resound through Heidegger's work, whether in the early lectures on Aristotle and *Being and Time,* or in the later discourses and dialogues, all which seem to revolve around, or at least echo, a central theme of surrender, or *lassen.* In *Contributions,* Heidegger warns us, numerous times, that it will not be enough to think our way towards a new beginning. Indeed, a new beginning requires a beginning without words precisely because

> Words fail us; they do so originally and not merely occasionally, whereby some discourse or assertion could indeed be carried out but is left unuttered, i.e., where the saying of something sayable or the re-saying of something already said is simply not carried through. Words do not yet come

---

12   Ibid.
13   Ibid.

to speech at all, but it is precisely in failing us that they arrive at the first leap. This failing is the event as intimation and intrusion of Being.[14]

Being comes forward in the space between words, between constructed thoughts. Heidegger does not discuss nonthinking *per se,* but as has already pointed out in "What Calls for Thinking," that which is most thought-provoking is "that we are still not thinking."[15] That this kind of thinking — the thinking of the scientific, rational world — and the thinking of nonthinking — are deeply different is made brilliantly clear in the above quotation. By words failing us, by allowing ourselves to wander or be carried to the edge of the abyssal beyond, our thinking has brought us to that point whereby words cannot save us, and we achieve the point where, at least to Wittgenstein, "one must be silent."[16] This silence is the "intimation of [...] Being," the coming to the fore of the unnameable, of the primordial silence that *be-*comes.

In Heidegger's "Memorial Address" from 1955, he discusses the difficulty of attuning oneself to the new thinking towards the new beginning which he has already discussed in *Contributions.* While careful not to dismiss entirely "calculative thinking" (he says that both are indeed needed), it is "meditative thinking" that the "contemporary" human being is in flight from. The contemporary human being too often eschews the pause and the space that true thinking requires. This is not to say that inventiveness and industry are not happening, only that reflective thinking — meditative thinking — escapes one who is too committed to "progress." In response to the criticism that meditative thinking both "loses touch" and is "worthless for dealing

---

14 Martin Heidegger, *Contributions to Philosophy (Of the Event),* trans. Richard Rojcewicz and Daniela Vallega-Neu (Bloomington: Indiana University Press, 2012), 30.

15 Heidegger, *Basic Writings,* 370.

16 The full quoatation, as the final line of Wittgenstein's *Tractatus Loigico-philosophicus,* reads "Whereof one cannot speak, thereof one must remain silent." (Ludwig Wittgenstein, *Tractatus Loigico-philosophicus,* trans. C.K. Ogden [New York, Harcourt, Brace & Company, 1922], 189).

with [...] business" as well as being "above the reach of ordinary understanding," Heidegger advises that to achieve this meditative pause requires practice. "At times," he says, "it requires a greater effort. It demands more practice. It is in need of even more delicate care than any other genuine craft."[17] Thinking here is a craft, and a craft requires training. It requires a practice, a training towards thinking, and yet, science, as a calculating, amassing form-of-thinking denies thinking even this. In the "Address," Heidegger says that this type of thinking need not be "high-flown." Rather, "it is enough if we dwell on what lies close and meditate on what is closest; upon that which concerns us, each one of us, here and now."[18] Though he does not say this explicitly, we can hear the echo of Dōgen when he advises, in the "Genjōkōan" that this "inexhaustible store" — this closest of worlds is "present right beneath our feet and within a single drop of water."[19]

The practice of meditation for Heidegger first requires a willingness to let go, to *lassen*. Heidegger describes the process of letting-go in relation to technology as a "releasement toward things" (*Die Gelassenheit zu den Dingen*). We must, he seems to be saying, hold technology very loosely; we must use it to build where we dwell, but also "deny [it] the right to dominate us." While this address focuses on the danger of becoming seduced by technology (to the detriment of that other form of thinking), we can see that Heidegger is also pointing us towards something else. He says in the "Address":

Releasement towards things and openness to the mystery belong together. They grant us the possibility of dwelling in the world in a totally different way. They promise us a new ground and foundation upon which we can stand and endure in the world of technology without being imperiled by it.[20]

17 Martin Heidegger, *Discourse on Thinking,* trans. John M. Anderson and E. Hans Freund (New York: Harper & Row, 1966), 47.
18 Ibid.
19 Ibid., 43.
20 Ibid., 55.

To open ourselves to the mystery of *be*-coming, to the mystery of Being's incipient arrival, first requires a releasing of the certainty of being. To locate ourselves on a new ground means we must first abandon the other, old ground, entirely. This movement returns us, if briefly, to the horror of the leap; there is a letting go here, and to let go fully means to risk, or even to welcome utter abandonment, to find oneself alone (as absolute emptiness). This abandonment is dealt with extensively by Heidegger in *Contributions*; he describes the abandonment as "the forgottenness of being and the breakdown of truth."[21] These, Heidegger writes, are essentially the same thing, yet each must be deeply thought, each "be brought to meditation."[22] It is much safer never to think what Heidegger calls the "plight," but this plight, the greatest plight that is "the lack of a sense of plight in the midst of this plight,"[23] must be thought — thinking here *becomes* the leap, a leap necessary to break through the rigid, ossified world *we still inhabit*.

For Heidegger then, the practice of thinking is a surrender of the certainty of being to the precisely uncertain nature of *be*-coming. Becoming transforms being from the concrete, knowable, absolute into the uncertain flowing of becoming, and with this transformation, everything changes. Nothing is authentically known if knowing is a learning of facts; this acquisition of knowledge is always seizing, a taking, a naming; if knowing (as opposed to knowledge; the verb in a state of action versus the staid noun) is instead a thinking-towards *be*-coming, a knowing that is allowed to become anything (even *no*thing), then knowing becomes an active practice, thought becomes a taking-up of thinking.

Out of this taking up, for Heidegger, arises a sudden "resonating," a *be*-coming of everything. Being is abandoned as a certainty and in its wake vibrant life as epitomized by a resonating of all becomings takes place. This vibrant life — what Heidegger

---

21 Heidegger, *Contributions to Philosophy (Of the Event)*, 90.

22 Ibid.

23 Ibid.

calls lived experience — emerges in the abyssal in between, providing, if not the certainty of something new, then at least the possibility of a new arrival, a new *be*-coming.

Practice *qua* Practice

Nishitani echoes Heidegger's thinking *towards* when he describes the non-knowing of Buddhist practice as "a field that goes beyond consciousness and intellect."

It would have to be a field of *śūnyatā* or emptiness, appearing as the field of a wisdom we might call a "knowing of non-knowing." From this field we could even take a second look at conscious or intellectual knowing and see it reduced finally to the "knowing of not-knowing." Similarly, it would be a field of praxis that might be called an "action of non-action," whence we could take a second look at all our activity and see it as nothing other than an "action of non-action." And lastly, it would be a standpoint where knowledge and praxis are one, a field where things would become manifest in their own suchness.[24]

This non-knowing becomes known through the practice of deep, careful thinking, through an examination of the inherent emptiness of a world and by an elimination of the "false views" that crowd our knowing with false claims to beingness. The non-knowing of knowing becomes known through the practice of *samādhi,* or, as Nishitani writes later, "where the self can be absolutely itself." This is a point where "the eye does not see the eye, fire does not burn fire [...], where the willows are not green and the flowers are not red, [... at this point] it withdraws beyond all reason and *logos*."[25] World drops away, like Dōgen's body-and-mind, to a point of stillness — withdrawn but absolutely present — a space or clearing of no thing which welcomes all into it as possibility, as a resonating.

---

24 Keiji Nishitani, *Religion and Nothingness,* trans. Jan Van Bragt (Berkeley: University of California Press, 1982), 122.

25 Ibid., 188.

For Dōgen, thinking becomes a practice when we take up a sustained sitting practice — for there can be no substitute — but it is also possible for the practice to be taken up as the everyday, from moment to moment. For Dōgen, "[w]e should continue in this way even further, because practice and realization, and for all that is possessed of life, it is the same."[26] There is an emphasis on work as a practice, and within, the Buddhist tradition, the eight-fold noble path is just that, a *Holzweg towards* and not a level achieved.

For Heidegger, practice *qua* practice is not so clear. He favors a withdrawal, a stepping back clearly, but does not offer a guide towards a sustained, defined practice, beyond the practice of the leap. Through an authentic experience of the uncovering of truth as *alētheia,* through a willingness to leap into the uncertainty which rests (or doesn't) between the banks of certainty, we are able to experience the world *as it is,* in the form(s) of a new beginning becoming again, but on the subject of how one is prepare for that leap, things are less clear.

Perhaps what comes through most clearly as a *practice* for Heidegger, as a stepping away from the seeing of *theōria* and into the doing of *praxis,* is for a "taking up" of the practice of withdrawal itself, an act of refusal towards the the given world, the world into which one has always already been thrown into. This stepping back, or letting go, is a "waiting." In waiting we refuse to name, we *cannot* name (for to name would be to reify); rather we must wait "because waiting releases itself into the openness [...] into the expanse of distance [...] in whose nearness it finds the abiding in which remains."[27] And so we wait, *as a practice,* and for Heidegger, that practice takes place in a "simple solitude."

> For what matters is to know that here, in all barrenness and frightfulness, something of the essence of Being is resonating and the abandonment of beings (as machination and lived

---

26 Dōgen, *The Heart of Dōgen's Shōbōgenzō,* 44.

27 Heidegger, *Discourse on Thinking,* 68.

experience) by Being is dawning. This age of questioning can be overcome only by an age of that simple solitude in which a readiness for the truth of Being is prepared.[28]

This age of the simple solitude, this age in which the retreat from the clamor of being in technology seems so important, this time of waiting *as a practice,* seems to me the closest we can come to following Heidegger's idea to the limit. He refuses to claim an answer, to make an absolute. He leaves us in silence, in the graceful — and attentive — waiting of the prisoners' dialogue. Heidegger ends *Contributions* with a small series of paragraphs on language. In them, he describes that language both humanizes and dehumanizes human beings. He writes that "language is grounded in silence."[29] Perhaps it is by embodying this practice of listening to the silence *as a practice* that we can find the clearing through which being comes, finally, to Being.

---

28 Heidegger, *Contributions to Philosophy (Of the Event),* 87.
29 Ibid., 401.

Conclusion

With(in) the Hyper-Event

What this reading of Heidegger and Dōgen has so far attempted has been to investigate the subjects of ontology and epistemology as dialogically placed between Heidegger and Dōgen, and as a conversation between the East and the West, seeking not so much similarities and differences but forms of possibilities, beginnings, potential traversals. The subject has been, as already mentioned, treated *irresponsibly*. To anyone immersed in the thinking of the West or of the East, there remain clear, decisive differences between the two traditions, and to reading one against the other is to take liberties, to bend the rules, to ignore obvious contradictions. This study has been a reaction against the sensible, against the logical, and against, precisely, the ossified practices of a philosophy practiced — too often — as the "regulated-regulating instruments of information."[1] This reading of Heidegger and Dōgen therefore is meant to be seen with humor, or at least, if not that, to be treated with a certain speculative lightness, to be read with a smile — perhaps — and a bearing which welcomes the possibilities proposed here. To hew too closely to an already claimed world is potentially to miss the possibility of an *other* world. The opening of possibilities are

---

1   Heidegger, *Basic Writings,* 434.

practiced, with Heidegger, in the taking of a leap into an abyssal between, in surrendering oneself into the potentiality "a new beginning," or in, with Dōgen, the "falling away" of mind-and-body. Reacting to a long period of stagnation in thinking, in which instrumental, formulaic responses seem to have replaced the simple awe and wonder of the thinking of the primordial that remains the wonder of original thinking, I desire in this study no less than to invite new directions forwards, or *towards,* seeing and understanding the two major thinkers investigated here. I do this not to offer one more interpretation of Heidegger or Dōgen, one more studied tome; there are others better qualified for that undertaking. In this study, I respond to the imprecation towards the creative; I respond to that *creatively.* In both thinkers, I see in their strikingly original thinking a way *out* of the crisis — whether environmental, personal or otherwise (though always existential) — in which we find ourselves drifting inexorably towards.

Like Blanchot stumbling from near certain execution before the firing line into a dark forest filled with burning fires,[2] we have treated this writing as an attempt *to get beyond* the irradiated fires of scientific, rational thinking which burn brightly around us, to take Heidegger at his word and to expose ourselves, and to leap — recklessly — into the abyssal between. As Heidegger writes in *Contributions,* "the basic disposition of thinking in the other beginning oscillates within shock, restraint, diffidence."[3] In *shock* we have opened ourselves to the possibility of something other, something which exceeds (*always, already*) that which has been presented to us, a truth which resonates beyond that granted us by a society which is resistant to — even deeply horrified by — the possibility of change, or a new beginning; in *restraint,* we have attempted to *practice* that "hesitant self-withholding," that holding back of named being in order to allow

2   Maurice Blanchot, *The Instant of My Death,* trans. Elizabeth Rottenberg (Stanford: Stanford University Press, 2000), 4.

3   Martin Heidegger, *Contributions to Philosophy (Of the Event),* trans. Richard Rojcewicz and Daniela Vallega-Neu (Bloomington: Indiana University Press, 2012), 14.

to come forth what is so far unknown and withdrawn. Practicing *restraint* allows for a new, inceptual thinking to take place, a thinking which draws us *towards the already withdrawn.* In *diffidence* as well, practiced as hesitancy, as a form of respect, we have sought to *be*-come near, to expose ourselves, as authentic beings, to the thinking of the new beginning.

More importantly, and pressingly, this study has been a project towards divining a way forward towards the possibilities begun in the thinking of Heidegger and Dōgen (and less so Nishitani) and has been conducted in the glare of potential ecological cataclysm and social disintegration. Since this projects inception, we have seen the collapse of the Larsen B ice shelf in Antartica, and the opening up of Northern shipping routes across a routinely ice-free Arctic (and the expectation that the Arctic will be entirely ice free by 2020, a fact celebrated with jubilation by at least one Northeastern United States governor.) Super storm Sandy personally affected me and millions more, while Super Typhoon Haiyan resulted in utter devastation in the Philippines, killing over 6,000 in a single day with millions displaced. The super as a descriptive in the storm seems to hearken to an event which begins to exceed language; will there come soon a "super-super" Typhoon? In Australia, a drought has wreaked havoc for years on the region, resulting in massive crop loss and tremendous brush fires which annually scorch thousands of square miles, killing dozens. In 2003, a heat wave in Northern Europe caused an estimated 25,000 to 70,000 deaths, and in 2010 in Russia, an extreme heat wave led to hundreds of forest fires which burned across the region for months and resulted directly in over 100 deaths; however, indirectly the corresponding heat-related fatalities killed over 56,000. As I write, a heat wave in India, with daytime temperatures exceeding 48 degrees Celsius, is estimated to have killed 2,000 already with little sign of it abating anytime soon. The war in Syria, resulting in nearly 700,000 deaths so far and a region catastrophically destabilized, with millions displaced, and conflict now spreading across the Arabian peninsula, and into the African continent, stems from an orange seller's frustration in Tunisia at rising food prices, the result of a warming climate which saw food shortages across the globe; that year, 2011, saw food riots in no less than 36 countries. In California, again as I write, a drought once thought to be the "drought of a decade" has quickly become the "drought of a century" and recently has been referred to as the "drought of the millennium." This is not mere Weather Channel marketing; California has never seen in its recorded history its reservoirs so depleted, and this spring it was widely reported that the state had less than a year of water left in reserve.[4] The list unfortunately goes on.

This is horrifying. It is terrifying. It resists a response. The temptation to turn away is natural, to immerse oneself in the minutia of one's life — swim team, soccer practice, departmental meetings, Downton Abbey, the latest iPhone 6, 7, 8, 9, 10… (the list must go on) and the corresponding os updates preoccupy one, *distract* one. To *dis-tract* means to be pulled asunder, to be drawn away from; with Heidegger then, we can read that to be *distracted* by the latest technological bibelot is in fact to be "drawn away" from that which draws near. The climate emergency emerges into our consciousness as a call; we can answer that call, thinking the possibilities that unfold in that call. We can also turn away, and become pulled asunder. Unlike previous crises, such as the threat of nuclear annihilation or global war in which our faith was placed, albeit with skepticism, with the "rational" actors of national governments, the threat of climate change, or global warming, seems inexorable. We know what we must do, *yet we turn away.* In 1996 in a response to a series of riots across France, Jean-luc Nancy wrote a brief essay in which he stated that our only response to a world falling apart, the response that was most pressing, was to raise the question "what is to be done?" The question, he writes, is on everyone's lips but remains "withheld, barely uttered for we do not even know if we still have the right, or whether we have the means,

---

4   In Cape Town, South Africa, Day Zero (the day in which the city of nearly 4 million will run out of water) is only ever just barely deferred, existing as a constant possibility.

to raise it."[5] We do not even raise the question, and in not raising the question, we turn away, we do not even begin to think that which is most terrifying, most horrifying. In Heidegger's essay "What Calls for Thinking?" he writes that what is "*most thought provoking is that we are still not thinking*— not even yet, although the state of the world is becoming constantly more thought-provoking."[6] Echoing Heidegger and Nancy, we can only demand that the only true response, the only true beginning, is to turn to face the crisis, to *raise the question* and to take up the task of thinking once again. To start. Again.

In March, 2011, a 9.0 earthquake, now called the Tōhuku earthquake, devastated Japan. For six minutes, buildings shook and crumbled, highways buckled and bridges collapsed. Subsequently, a tsunami drenched the Fukushima Daiichi nuclear plant in Japan, resulting in, along with over 20,000 deaths, an uncontrolled meltdown (and possibly even a "melt-through")[7] of three of its six reactors. In the ensuing cataclysm, the nuclear plant unleashed a toxic spume of radioactive gases into the atmosphere (as well as, in the subsequent years, substantial amounts of highly contaminated water directly into the ocean.) That day, Japan experienced three "events" but the word "Fukushima" has come to represent everything that happened that day, and since. In *Hyperobjects,* Timothy Morton refers to the radioactive isotopes released in Fukushima (and in Chernobyl, Three Mile Island, Hiroshima, Nagasaki, and countless atomic bomb tests, nuclear accidents, as well as still unknown and undisclosed releases of radioactive material) as hyperobjects. Morton uses *hyper* to describe how an object — a thing in the world — supersedes and exceeds our understanding of it;

---

5   Jean-Luc Nancy and Phillipe Lacoue-Labarthe, *Retreating the Political,* ed. Simon Sparks (London: Routledge, 1997), 191.

6   Martin Heidegger, *Basic Writings,* ed. David Farrell Krell (New York: Harper & Row, 1977), 371.

7   Sara B. Pritchard, "An Envirotechnical Disaster: Negotiating Nature, Technology and Politics at Fukushima," in *Japan at Nature's Edge,* eds. Ian Jared Miller, Julia Adeny Thomas, Brett L. Walker (Honolulu: University of Hawaii Press, 2013), 256.

the thing, in Morton's words — *viscous, nonlocal,* and *interobjective* — moves beyond our understanding, irreducible always to a single *thing* in the world. While we commonly think of *hyper* colloquially as referring to speed, Morton draws on the etymological roots of the word, *hyper-* and refers to an element which is "over," or "beyond." For Morton, the thing, whether a radioactive isotope or a plastic bag, a cosmic universe or a mere nuclear explosion is hyper in that it is "over," or "beyond" our capabilities to grasp it in its entirety.

In the case of the nuclear meltdown at the Fukushima Dai-ichi plant, the entire unravelling might just as well be called a *hyperevent,* an event so far beyond our capacity to understand that it exceeds categories. The word Fukushima comes to stand in for an unravelling, mis-understood event, clouded in its own eventing and one that can never be fully understood, nor even *experienced.* To term an event *hyper* (rather than a mere object) is to understand that the event itself in its *eventing* is never finished; the hyperevent continues to unfold in ways unimaginable, or more importantly, unthought, to us. Where did the accident of Fukushima happen? Most clearly at the plant itself, but it also has a way of spreading, unfolding, *be-*coming in a way that is never finished. Certainly there is a clear causal link between the 9.0 earthquake that happened offshore, and the resulting tsunami which caused the waters to rise so precipitously (in one bay the wave was measured at over 38 meters) flooding and disabling the plant, leading to the meltdown. But could we trace the event — the actual hyper-event itself — back to when the plant was built? Or further to the Manhattan project of World War Two or the Trinity test site in southern New Mexico, site of the first nuclear explosion? Or to the thinking of a community which places the risk of a nuclear accident at less than zero? And when does the "hyperevent" of the Fukushima disaster end? According to a press release from the Physicians for Social Responsibility, cesium-137 has a half-life of thirty years, and "since it takes about ten half-lives for any radionuclide to disappear" it will literally take centuries before the exclusion zone becomes habitable again. And even then, will the hyperevent have exhausted itself, or simply reached a new manifestation? The point of the hyperevent, as with Morton's hyperobject, is that we just don't know; the event and object, as we draw closer to understanding them, draw farther away; the event itself becomes stranger the closer we get to it; the event, in its eventing, is uncanny.

Global warming as the result of unprecedented climate change is the preternatural hyperevent of our time; it remains impossible to understand when it began, and how, and even more impossible to determine the various ways in which it will continue to unfold. The cause seems to lie most obviously in our burning of carbon emitting fuels, whether via our factories, our jets or our cars, and seems to accelerate with the dawn of the Industrial Revolution. It continues apace, however, even as the Industrial Revolution seems to foreclose on itself. Will anthropogenic climate change lead to the death of humanity, or only to the demise of Western culture, to a culture based on consumption, on profiteering and on exploitation? Will it result in death for everyone, or only for a small subset of humanity — Pacific Islanders, for instance, or Bangladeshis — peoples far removed, for the most part, from our own experiences? Will other societies arise in its wake, societies which are more resilient, more adaptable? What does sea level change look like? It seems ridiculous to fear a few inches, yet a few meters seems unimaginable. What happens to the 19 million residents of Florida (much closer to those of us in the West than the distant Bangladeshis) in the event of a single meter rise (which now seems inevitable) in ocean levels? What do we do with them? How do our understandings of justice or private property or capitalism change with an onset of human migration unlike what the world has ever seen? To a certain extent we are already seeing the effects of cataclysmic climate change in the bodies of migrants washed up on the beaches of the Mediterranean and the challenges this has brought to traditional European Enlightenment values. The rise of right wing parties across liberal democracies, whether exemplified by Greece's neo-Fascist New Dawn Party or Donald Trump, seem linked — albeit predictably — as emerging reactions to the environmental crisis; what must be *our* response to *them*? *Theirs* to *us*? How are we to go forward when the society, and the claimed values that built it, seem more and more to be but a sham, a mere Potemkin culture, or a disappearing mirage of good will?

These questions not only resist easy answers; *they resist all answers.* We think, as Heidegger has written, "in too limited a fashion." The questions that the hyperevent (as well as the hyperobject) provoke, require a new thinking, one unleashed from formulaic, rote, ratiocinative responses; it requires a new practice of thinking, an explosion towards what is unknown, what cannot be known, at least not yet, and to admit that they cannot be known. *Yet the effort must be made.* The questions behind the headlines — the thinking that has not yet been thought — acts as an irruption in the thinking which happens everyday. The questions themselves destroy the answers, and we accept this destruction happily. *For what stands now cannot continue.*

As global warming continues to become an accepted norm across the globe, governments and industry seek to capitalize on it in an almost gleeful way. Politicized and polarized, the chance for dialogue or for true thinking seems long past, and indeed even eclipsed by the drunken celebrations at the end of time (or history). What this reading has attempted to take up is the challenge posed by Heidegger and Dōgen to *see differently,* to attune ourselves to the possibility of something *other*. As Heidegger writes in "What Calls For Thinking," "There is no bridge here — only the leap."[8] We cannot plan for the transition; rather it must be a falling, a willful plunging into the abyssal between. We must trust the leap, or at least trust that *this* cannot stand anymore. In *Contributions,* Heidegger writes that the leap "appears in the semblance of utter recklessness" and yet precisely it is this recklessness — this irresponsibility — which allows for the opening of being to the event. He writes, "before all else,

---

8   Heidegger, *Basic Writings,* 373.

[the leap] leaps into the belonging to Being in the full essential occurrence of Being as event."[9]

What the question posed by the unfolding event of the environmental crisis takes up requires a radical, even reckless, response; it must admit to, as Nancy wrote in "What Is To Be Done?" asking questions which leave the world "perpetually reopened, of its own contradiction."[10] We must, he continues, "act in such a way that this world is a world able to open itself up to its own uncertainty as such."[11]

The Task Rethought...

What I have attempted to do here is to read both Heidegger through Dōgen, and Dōgen through Heidegger. This is an act of irresponsibility — recklessness at best, futility at worst — and one which presupposes an authority I lack, and which I doubt, with Heidegger and Dōgen, truly exists. For me, philosophy works best on the leading edge of the creative; indeed, the creative thinking towards wisdom can only lead to the love of wisdom, the *sophos* of thinking. Though unmentioned, there is an aspect of the Deleuzian gesture in this reading; the hope is that, through a creative reading with Heidegger and Dōgen, we are able to traverse and open out a new line of thinking, one which, as already mentioned, and though still unidentified, has within it the potential to change, or alter, the general direction in which society finds itself drifting. In Deleuze and Guattari's *What Is Philosophy?*, they claim that "philosophy is the discipline that involves *creating* concepts."[12] A discipline is as much a practice as anything else, and it is within this practice of *creation,* of conceiving and thinking *something* else, that I seek, and which I find, in Heidegger's demands. Derrida also helps us on

9 Heidegger, *Contributions to Philosophy (Of the Event),* 179.

10 Jean-Luc Nancy and Phillipe Lacoue-Labarthe, *Retreating The Political,* ed. Simon Sparks (London: Routledge, 1997). 191.

11 Ibid.

12 Gilles Deleuze and Félix Guattari, *What Is Philosophy?,* trans. Hugh Tomlinson and Graham Burchell (New York: Columbia University Press, 1994): 16.

our way (*Holzweg*) describing deconstruction — thinking — as "inventive or nothing at all. [... I]t opens up a passageway, it marches ahead and marks a trail."[13] In his "Letter to a Japanese Friend," Derrida attempts to explain to a Japanese translator how to understand the word "deconstruction"; he writes that "deconstruction takes place, it is an event that does not await the deliberation, consciousness, or organization of a subject. [...] [I]t deconstructs itself."[14]

In *The End of Philosophy and the Task of Thinking,* Heidegger describes how philosophy, when taken over and coopted by the rational sciences, becomes foreclosed; he writes that the original project of philosophy, the essential questioning which hearkens us (back) towards authentic being becomes lost, occluded, dismembered by the logical, ratiocinated faculties of the sciences. The late Pierre Hadot named this original questioning the "wonder of philosophy." This wondering becomes an active refusal to be set upon by the logic of the sciences; it is awe, it is bafflement, it is a political and metaphysical stance to refuse the known, the categorizable. In wondering we seek not the answer — this would be too easy — but wonder itself. As an ontological and epistemological practice, it is the asking of the question *what is the nature of being?* as much as it is the seeking of an answer. In *The End of Philosophy,* Heidegger proposes that the demise of philosophy — a "triumph" for the "scientific-technological world" — can offer the possibility for a new kind of thinking, a kind of thinking that might appear after "the dissolution of philosophy in the technologized sciences."[15] This thinking, starkly opposed to the foreclosed, scholastic philosophy of the academy, offers a new path into and through the world. This thinking, freed from the sciences, "is content with awakening a readiness

13 Jacques Derrida, "Psyche: Inventions of the Other," in *Reading De Man Reading,* eda. Lindsay Waters and Wlad Godzich, trans. Catherine Porter and Phillip Lewis (Minneapolis: University of Minnesota Press, 1994), 42.

14 David Wood and Robert Bernasconi, eds., *Derrida and Différance* (Evanston: Northwestern University Press, 1988), 3.

15 Martin Heidegger, *Basic Writings,* ed. David Farrell Krell (New York: Harper & Row, 1977), 436.

in man for a possibility whose contour remains obscure, whose coming remains uncertain."[16] It is a thinking which is "preparatory," which resists prediction; it says what has already been said "a long time ago," but which "has not been explicitly thought."[17]

The issue of ontology — of what comes to be, and how it comes to be — is one of enormous importance; contained within it are the seeds of an ethical practice in which how we treat others, how we treat the planet, and the very relations between things, are brought to the fore as a questioning and a thinking that is so very necessary in a world that "has not yet begun to think." These things frankly matter very much. For too long, as Heidegger explains, philosophy has become the handmaiden of instrumentalization, taking a subsidiary role to the creative act, to the act born from an authentic thinking practiced within the clearing of the primordial ground. What philosophy needs then is to let loose at times, to fall away from the sphere of logic and rationality, from formulas and predictable outcomes. In a very real sense, we do not know that much more about ourselves, or of our cosmos, than when Heraclitus first gazed upon his river, or when Diogenes the Dog turned his head away from Alexander the Great. Certainly, we have been to the moon, and created munitions capable of destroying the planet thousands of times over (one often wonders about this figure; does it matter if a weapon can destroy the planet any more times than once? And for whom is it destroyed? Is the landscape which flourishes in the no man's land surrounding Chernobyl really destroyed? Again, for whom?) We have healed billions and improved without a doubt the lives of even more. And yet, despite all our sciences and explanations, we cannot explain the most fundamental question of being. We return again and again to it, and yet, like all things, especially thoughts, it resists an answer.

The resistance to an easy answer, indeed to any answer, is an uncomfortable position to take in philosophy, as it is in life. It leaves one on the margin, living just beyond the *periphérique*,

---

16   Ibid.
17   Ibid.

on the outskirts of the city, the city society has built, and from which one is permanently excluded. This exclusion is felt keenly, for no matter how much one moves away from the center, the center entices, it attracts. As Jean-Luc Nancy and Aurélien Barrau write in *What's These Worlds Coming To?* resistance finds its genesis in a rebellion against society's unquestioning, "obsessive," embrace with ontological order and a "recurrent phobia of dis-order."[18] The world as conceived by society demands a structured, hierarchical regime in which questions are answered *before* they are asked, that what is unknown is quickly occluded by the proven, by the claimed fact. Nancy and Barrau write:

> To truly enter into the disorder, to explore its crevices, to climb out onto its branches, to get drenched by its tumultuous downpour, perhaps one would need to return to the technological aporia that pushes one — that compels one — to no longer fear the disorderly and the irreversible, and finally, that orders or enjoins one to leave the entropic phobia behind.[19]

To fall into the disorder, then, requires a leap, a surrender, a falling away. Not everyone is willing to take that up. Not everyone is able. Indeed, for Heidegger, it is *only the rare, only the few* who will ever attempt the leap.

But it is for them this world, for those who leap.

---

18 Jean-Luc Nancy and Aurélian Barrau, *What's These Worlds Coming To?*, trans. Travis Holloway and Flor Méchain (New York: Fordham University Press, 2015), 69.

19 Ibid..

Bibliography

In lieu of a traditional bibliography, one that merely repeats citations that have already been mentioned within the text, this bibliography aims to catalogue all (or most) of the references I came across and read during the course of this project. While everything referenced in the text is cited here, there are publications here that are not referenced inside the book. These are whispers to hidden texts, haunted allusions, echoes even (though here, not of no thing, but of some thing).

Aristotle. *The Works of Aristotle.* Translated by W.D. Ross. Chicago: The University of Chicago, 1952.

Beckett, Samuel. *The Unnamable.* New York: Grove Press, 1958.

Bestegui, Miguel de. "Mindfulness (Besinnung)." *Notre Dame Philosophical Reviews.* https://ndpr.nd.edu/news/25281-mindfulness-besinnung/.

Blanchot, Maurice. *The Instant of My Death.* Translated by Elizabeth Rottenberg. Stanford: Stanford University Press, 2000.

———. *The Station Hill Blanchot Reader.* Translated by Lydia Davis, Paul Auster, and Robert Lamberton. Barrytown: Station Hill, 1999.

———. *The Writing of the Disaster.* Translated by Ann Smock. Lincoln: University of Nebraska, 1995.

Bodiford, William M. "Remembering Dōgen: Eiheiji and Dōgen Hagiography." *The Journal of Japanese Studies* 32, no. 1 (2006): 1–21. DOI: 10.1353/jjs.2006.0003.

Bredeson, Garrett Zantow. "On Dōgen and Derrida." *Philosophy East and West* 58, no. 1 (2008): 60–82. DOI: 10.1353/pew.2008.0009.

Capobianco, Richard. *Engaging Heidegger.* Toronto: University of Toronto, 2010.

Caputo, John D. *Demythologizing Heidegger.* Bloomington: Indiana University Press, 1993.

———. *Radical Hermeneutics: Repetition, Deconstruction and the Hermeneutic Project.* Bloomington: Indiana University Press, 1987.

Carter, Robert. *The Kyoto School: An Introduction.* New York: State University of New York Press, 2013.

Charles E. Scott, Susan M. Schoenbaum, Daniela Vallega-Neu, and Alejandro Vallega, eds. *Companion to Heidegger's Contributions to Philosophy.* Bloomington: Indiana University Press, 2001.

Cook, Francis. *Hua-Yen Buddhism: The Jewel Net of Indra.* University Park: The Pennsylvania University Press, 1977.

Critchley, Simon. *Infinitely Demanding: Ethics of Commitment, Politics of Resistance.* London & New York: Verso, 2007.

Davis, Bret W., Jason Wirth, and Brian Schroeder, eds. *Japanese and Continental Philosophy: Conversations with the Kyoto School.* Bloomington: Indiana University Press, 2011.

Deleuze, Gilles, and Félix Guattari. *What Is Philosophy?* Translated by Hugh Tomlinson and Graham Burchell. New York: Columbia University Press, 1994.

Derrida, Jacques. "Psyche: Inventions of the Other." In *Reading De Man Reading,* edited by Lindsay Waters and Wlad Godzich, translated by Catherine Porter and Phillip Lewis. Minneapolis: University of Minnesota Press, 1994.

Derrida, Jacques, and Maurizio Ferraris. *A Taste For The Secret.* Translated by Giacomo Donis. Cambridge: Polity, 2002.

Dōgen, Eihei. *The Heart of Dōgen's Shōbōgenzō.* Translated by Norman Waddell and Masao Abe. Albany: State University of New York Press, 2002.

Fynsk, Christopher. *Heidegger: Thought and Historicity.* Ithaca: Cornell University Press, 1986.

———. *Language and Relation: …That There Is Language.* Stanford: Stanford University Press, 1996.

———. *Last Steps: Maurice Blanchot's Exilic Writing.* New York: Fordham University Press, 2013.

Harman, Graham. "Dwelling with the Fourfold." *Speed and Culture* 12, no. 3 (August 2009): 292–302. DOI: 10.1177/1206331209337080.

———. *Heidegger Explained.* Chicago: Open Court, 2007.

———. *Tool Being: Heidegger and the Metaphysics of Objects.* Chicago: Open Court, 2002.

Hee-Jin Kim. *Eihei Dōgen: Mystical Realist.* Sommerville: Wisdom Publications, 2004.

Heidegger, Martin. *Basic Writings.* Edited by David Farrell Krell. New York: Harper & Row, 1977.

———. *Being and Time.* Translated by John Macquarrie and Edward Robinson. New York: Harper & Row, 1962.

———. *Beiträge zur Philosophie (Vom Ereignis).* Frankfurt am Main: Vittorio Klostermann, 2003.

———. *Contributions to Philosophy (From Enowning).* Translated by Parvis Emad and Kenneth Maly. Bloomington: Indiana University Press, 1999.

———. *Contributions to Philosophy (Of the Event).* Translated by Richard Rojcewicz and Daniela Vallega-Neu. Bloomington: Indiana University Press, 2012.

———. *Country Path Conversations.* Translated by Bret W. Davis. Bloomington: Indiana University Press, 2010.

———. *Discourse on Thinking.* Translated by John M. Anderson and E. Hans Freund. New York: Harper & Row, 1966.

———. *Four Seminars.* Bloomington: Indiana University Press, 2003.

———. *History of the Concept of Time Prolegomena.* Translated Theodore Kiesel. Indianapolis: Indiana University Press, 1985.

———. *Mindfulness.* Translated by Parvis Emad and Thomas Kalary. London:New York: Continuum International, 2006.

———. *Nietzsche Volume II: The Eternal Recurrence of the Same.* Translated by David Farrell Krell. San Francisco: Harper & Row, 1984.

———. *On the Way to Language.* New York: Harper & Row, 1971.

———. *On Time and Being.* Translated by Joan Stambaugh. New York: Harper & Row, 1972.

———. *Poetry, Language, Thought.* Translated by Albert Hofstadter. New York: Harper & Row, 1971.

———. *The Concept of Time.* Translated by Ingo Farin. London: Continuum, 2011.

———. *The Event.* Translated by Richard Rojcewicz. Bloomington: Indiana University Press, 2013.

———. *What Is Called Thinking?* Translated by J. Glenn Gray. New York: Harper & Row, 1968.

Heine, Steven. *A Dream within a Dream, Vol. V: Asian Thought and Culture.* New York: Peter Lang, 1991.

_____. *The Existential and Ontological Dimensions of Time in Heidegger and Dōgen.* Albany: State University of New York Press, 1985.

———. "Beyond Personal Identity: Dōgen, Nishida, and a Phenomenology of No-Self (review)." *Philosophy East and West* 54, no. 4 (2004): 569–71. DOI: 10.1353/pew.2004.0029.

———. ed. *Dōgen: Textual and Historical Studies.* Oxford: Oxford University Press, 2012.

Heisig, James W. *Philosophers of Nothingness.* Honolulu: University of Hawai'i Press, 2001.

Kierkegaard, Søren. *Fear And Trembling: Repetition.* Translated by Howard V. Hong and Edna H. Hong. Princeton: Princeton University Press, 1983.

———. *The Concept of Anxiety: A Simple Psychologically Orienting Deliberation on the Dogmatic Issue of Hereditary Sin.* Translated by Reidar Thomte. Princeton: Princeton University Press, 1980.

Kim, Hee-Jin. *Dōgen on Meditation and Thinking: A Reflection on His View of Zen.* Albany: State University of New York Press, 2006.

Leighton, Dan, and Shohaku Okumura. *Dōgen's Extensive Record: A Translation of the Eihei Kōroku*. Boston: Wisdom Publications, 2010.

Luchte, James. *Heidegger's Early Philosophy: The Phenomenology of Ecstatic Temporality*. New York: Continuum International Publishing, 2008.

McGinn, Bernard. *The Mystical Thought of Meister Eckhart: The Man From Whom God Hid Nothing*. New York: Crossroads Publishing, 2001.

Mitchell, Andrew J. *The Fourfold: Reading the Late Heidegger*. Evanston: Northwestern Press University, 2015.

Morton, Timothy. *Ecology without Nature: Rethinking Environmental Aesthetics*. Cambridge: Harvard University Press, 2007.

———. *Hyperobjects: Philosophy and Ecology After the End of the World*. Minneapolis: University of Minnesota Press, 1991. 2013.

Nāgārjuna. *The Fundamental Wisdom of The Middle Way: Nāgārjuna's Mūlamadhyamakakārika*. Translated by Jay L. Garfield. New York: Oxford University Press, 1995.

Nancy, Jean-Luc. *The Inoperative Community*. Translated by Peter Conner, Lisa Garbus, Michael Holland, and Simona Sawhney. Minneapolis: University of Minnesota Press, 1991.

——— and Phillipe Lacoue-Labarthe. *Retreating The Political*. Edited by Simon Sparks. Warwick Studies in European Philosophy. London: Routledge, 1997.

——— and Aurélian Barrau. *What's These Worlds Coming To?* New York: Fordham University Press, 2015.

National Research Council of the National Academies. *Health Risks from Exposure to Low Levels of Ionizing Radiation: BEIR VII Phase 2*. Washington, DC: The National Academies Press, 2006. http://www.nap.edu/openbook.php?isbn=030909156X.

Nietzsche, Friedrich. *The Gay Science*. Translated by Walter Kaufman. New York: Random House, 1974.

Nishida, Kitaro. *An Inquiry into the Good.* Translated by Masao Abe and Christopher Ives. New Haven: Yale University Press, 1987.

Nishitani, Keiji. *Religion and Nothingness.* Translated by Jan Van Bragt. Berkeley: University of California Press, 1982.

———. *The Self Overcoming of Nihilism.* New York: State University of New York Press, 1990.

Okumura, Shohaku. *Realizing Genjokoan: The Key to Dōgen's Shobogenzo.* Sommerville: Wisdom Publications, 2010.

Olson, Carl. *Zen and the Art of Postmodern Philosophy.* New York: State University of New York Press, 2000.

Pessoa, Fernando. *The Book of Disquiet.* Translated by Richard Zenith. New York: Penguin Classics, 2002.

Polt, Richard. *Heidegger: An Introduction.* Ithaca: Cornell University Press, 1999.

Priest, Graham. *Beyond the Limits of Thought.* Oxford: Oxford University Press, 2002.

Pritchard, Sara B. "An Envirotechnical Disaster: Negotiating Nature, Technology and Politics at Fukushima." In *Japan at Nature's Edge,* edited by Ian Jared Miller, Julia Adeny Thomas, Brett L. Walker, 255–79. Honolulu: University of Hawai'i Press, 2013.

Raud, Rein. "'Place' and 'Being-Time': Spatiotemporal Concepts in the Thought of Nishida Kitarō and Dōgen Kigen." *Philosophy East and West* 54, no. 1 (2004): 29–51. DOI: 10.1353/pew.2003.0057.

———. "The Existential Moment: Rereading Dōgen's Theory of Time." *Philosophy East and West* 62, no. 2 (2012): 153–73. DOI: 10.1353/pew.2012.0033.

Stambaugh, Joan. *Impermanence Is Buddha-Nature: Dōgen's Understanding of Temporality.* Honolulu: University of Hawai'i Press, 1990.

———. *The Formless Self.* Albany: State University of New York Press, 1999.

Tanahashi, Kazuaki, ed. *The Treasury of the True Dharma Eye: Zen Master Dōgen's Shobo Genzo.* Boston: Shamballa Publications, 2010.

Vallega-Neu, Daniela. *Heidegger's* Contributions to Philosophy: *An Introduction.* Bloomington: Indiana University Press, 2003.

Von Uexküll, Jacob. *A Foray into the Worlds of Animals and Humans.* Translated by Joseph O'Neil. Minneapolis: University of Minnesota Press, 2010.

Ward, Karl. *Augenblick: The Concept of the "Decisive Moment" in 19th and 20th Century Western Philosophy.* Ashgate Publishing Limited, 2008.

Weinrich, Harold. *Lethe: The Art and Critique of Forgetting.* Translated by Steven Rendall. New York: Cornell University Press, 2004.

Wittgenstein, Ludwig. *Tractatus Loigico-philosophicus.* Translated by C.K. Ogden. New York, Harcourt, Brace & Company, 1922.

Wood, David, and Robert Bernasconi, eds. *Derrida and Différance.* Evanston: Northwestern University Press, 1988.

40901203R00115